marHaba

مرحبا

A Course in Levantine Arabic

Lebanese Dialect

George Nicolas El-Hage, Ph.D.

About the Cover: **Dabke** (Arabic: دبكة) is a modern Levantine Arab folk circle dance of possible Canaanite or Phoenician origin. It is popular in Palestine, Lebanon, Syria, Jordan, Turkey, and the northern region of Saudi Arabia. It is a form of both circle dance and line dancing and is widely performed at weddings and joyous occasions. The line forms from right to left. The leader of the *dabke* heads the line, alternating between facing the audience and the other dancers.

Dedication

To my wife, Mary Ann, who loves Lebanon, its culture, its language, and its people, and who inspired and encouraged me to write this book.

Table of Contents

Introduction

Levantine Dialect, sometimes also referred to as Syrian Dialect, is the oral, and in some instances, written form of speech used and is widely understood in the countries of the Levant: Lebanon, Syria, Jordan and Palestine. It is "written" because there is a massive body of literature, mainly poetry, written in dialect and published in magazines, books and periodicals. It is notable to mention that this poetry, mainly improvisation, "*irtijaal*," known as "*Zajal*," is recited orally on stage in a debate between two or more poets or at gatherings such as weddings, funerals, and national and social celebrations.

Zajal is the national register of the Lebanese culture and the collective memory of its literary history. This form of poetry mainly flourished, and still does, in Lebanon more than in any other Levantine or Arab country. Lebanese *Zajal* has its cherished tradition and unique heritage. It has its pioneers, rules, varieties, meters, and prosody, and is widely popular across the Middle East, and the *mahjar* world, wherever Lebanese and Arab nationals live and prosper in diaspora. Lebanese *Zajal* poets, as well as popular singers in Lebanese dialect, are constantly invited to perform across the Arab world and the West, which validates the assumption that the Levantine, particularly the Lebanese dialect, is widely understood and extremely popular in all countries where Arabic is spoken and understood in the world.

The Egyptian dialect is also widespread due to the large population of Egypt. Egypt is the largest and most populous Arab country. Its political influence and massive Egyptian workforce is pervasive across the Middle East. In addition,the successful Egyptian movie industry has popularized the Egyptian dialect and made it a household language across the Arab speaking world and North Africa.

Both Egyptian and Lebanese dialects are made even more popular in Europe and the Americas through the widespread media network of viewers that these two dialects enjoy. The successful satellite stations offer a variety of shows, movies, interviews and musicals that are broadcasted with liberal openness and minor censorship. Furthermore, the Middle East is of vital interest to the Western world in general, and to the United States in particular, as far as security and economic factors are concerned. The state of world affairs and current events testify to this fact and to the rapidly rising interest in mastering the Levantine dialect today.

Of course, one important factor that contributed so significantly to the popularity of both the Lebanese and Egyptian dialects, especially for native speakers at home and in diaspora, as well as for Arabic language speakers at large, is the plethora of popular songs and iconic singers and poets in both of these two dialects who are loved, cherished, emulated, idealized, watched and heard all over world. Some of the many famous names that readily come to mind are: SabaaH, Fairouz, Wadi ' al Safi, Sabaah Fakhri, Um Kulthum, 'abd al Wahhaab, Fareed al ATrash, 'abd al Haleem Hafez, the RaHbaani brothers, Zaghlul al Damour, Mousa Zughaib, Zayn Shu 'ayb, Talee ' Hamdaan, and countless others. These are Levantine and Egyptian singers and poets in *'ammiyya* (everyday speech) who elevated the spoken word to a level of unprecedented elegance, extreme popularity, and unsurpassed beauty.

Zajal[1] can be read or recited, but it is usually expected to be delivered orally and sung or chanted on stage. Although there are variations in pronunciation and vocabulary among the different flavors of the Levantine dialect spoken in the countries of the Levant, nevertheless, the commonalities that these four flavors of the Levantine dialect share form a unifying body of language that is, by far, more coherent and easily understood by all natives of this region also known as the "Fertile Crescent".

Linguistically speaking, it is important to mention that these variations, whether among the four flavors of Levantine dialect, or in comparison and contrast to Modern Standard Arabic, (MSA), which is a modified version of Classical Medieval Arabic, abound primarily on the lower level of vocabulary pertaining to basic survival needs, but as the discussion or level of conversation and discourse move up to higher levels on the (ILR) scale[2], upper 1+ and beyond, these differences

---

[1] George Nicolas El-Hage, "al zajal al lubnaani wa zaghloul al daamour fi beit meri" in *The Trilogy of Heroism, Redemption, and Triumph (Arabic Edition)* (San Bernardino: CreateSpace, 2014). (Available on amazon.com).

[2] The Interagency Language Roundtable (ILR) scale is a set of descriptions of abilities to communicate in a language. It is the standard grading scale for language proficiency in the Federal service. It was originally developed by the Interagency Language Roundtable (ILR), which included representation by United States Foreign Service Institute, the predecessor of the National Foreign Affairs Training Center (NFATC). It grades people's language proficiency on a scale of 0-5. The designation 0+, 1+, 2+, 3+, or 4+ is assigned when proficiency substantially exceeds one skill level and does not fully meet the criteria for the next level. This totals 11 possible grades. Grades may be assigned separately for different skills

almost dissipate. Just like in any other dialect, as you start to converse on levels 2 and 3 and deal with more sophisticated topics, you will have to start injecting more vocabulary that is common to both dialect and MSA and resort to code switching between dialect and Standard Arabic in order to get your message across.

It is arguably stated that by the very nature of its grammatical features, rich and sophisticated vocabulary, and linguistic structure, Levantine dialect is inherently closer to Modern Standard Arabic than other dialects in the region. While various dialects in the Middle East are used in the everyday speech of the natives and draw heavily on the oral tradition of the local region rather than on the written form of speech (no one uses MSA in daily conversation and survival needs), nevertheless, MSA remains the formal medium of expression in the press, news reporting, university lectures, formal speeches and official documents and announcements. You can safely say that people use dialect to speak every day and MSA to write and read. They do, however, listen in both MSA and dialect depending on the source and occasion. It is noticeable today that dialect is gaining solid grounds in becoming the norm in the media where films, plays, TV shows, news reporting and political Q&A sessions are all carried on in dialect.

The Arabic language is characterized by diglossia, which is the dichotomy between two forms of speech, formal and informal, written and oral. An Arab student, in any country of the Middle East, grows up speaking in the native dialect and later on learns MSA in school. Hence, dialect is the naturally acquired way of expressing one's self, while MSA

---

such as reading, speaking, listening, writing, translation, audio translation, interpretation, and intercultural communication.

is the formally learned means of communicating used in more formal situations. Dialect is the medium of communication which is not taught in schools; it is rather acquired at home by necessity and is spoken freely and orally to express immediate survival needs, feelings, emotions, desires, likes, dislikes, negotiations, buying and selling, arguing and debating, etc. It is simply what a child speaks until he (or she) goes to school. There, the child is introduced to the written alphabet, and consequently, moves on to formally read in MSA and learn the rules of grammar, infliction, voweling and spelling in addition to conjugation and more formal vocabulary.

Thus, a native Arab student learns MSA in school in a way similar to a foreign student learning Arabic in a foreign country. Of course, there are two major differences: First, the native student learns MSA at an earlier age, while a foreign university student at a Western university learns Arabic at a much older age, which poses a different set of issues for an adult learner to deal with, the affective filter being one of these serious hurdles.[3] Second, by the time the native student starts to learn MSA, his or her huge reservoir of already acquired vocabulary becomes a major contributor to fluency, an advantage that a foreign student is deprived of. In addition to learning new vocabulary, a foreign student will also have to learn grammar and syntax in order to function in Arabic as a new medium of communication.

---

[3] George Nicolas El-Hage, "A Communicative Approach to Teaching Arabic in Academia" in *Essays on Literature and Language* (San Bernardino: CreateSpace, 2014), p. 291. (Available on amazon.com).

However, my experience, as a long time teacher of Arabic to both native and non-native students has demonstrated to me that, with a few exceptions, while studying MSA, a native student may become more proficient and fluent in speaking, writing, and reading, but with less grammatical accuracy, while a foreign student continues to struggle with fluency but becomes more advanced as far as accuracy is concerned. While the native student relies on a huge base of vocabulary, better pronunciation and comprehension, he pays less attention to grammar as he takes it for granted that being a native gives him an advantage over non-native students in this respect. A foreign student, on the other hand, who struggles with vocabulary and proper pronunciation in comparison devotes more time to understanding grammatical rules and proper syntax which gives him a better advantage when writing and even testing in MSA.

It should also be stated that many native students struggle with Arabic grammar the same way the majority of foreign students do. So, being a native does not automatically, or necessarily, offer an immediate advantage, understanding or access to the complicated grammatical rules. You still have to be exposed to these rules, to consciously understand them, learn them, and ultimately acquire them, and be able to apply them at will and with the accuracy of an educated native speaker. This is one reason why many natives hesitate to converse in MSA, deliver a speech, grant an interview or even write a formal research paper unless they are specializing in Arabic language and literature. Knowing the grammatical rules and being able to explain them to students is a skill that even some teachers of Arabic, natives or not, do not possess. Hence, they pass on this weakness to their students who think that because they are non-natives, their knowledge of grammar is lacking, which is not the case.

This is not to say that dialects do not have grammar and rules of engagement, so to speak. But the fact remains that the native child would have already acquired, through immense practice, unconscious exposure, solid competency, and fluency, these rules that would have become a part of his consciousness. He would not have to consciously think about them in a mechanical way.

Similarly, the case of the heritage student could be made here as well. This is a child who was born to native Arab parents (or at least one parent) in a foreign country, and was taught Arabic (most likely a dialect) at home, through oral conversation. If lucky, the parent (s) would have insisted that the child should not only understand the message in Arabic, (or whatever the native language is), but that the child should respond in Arabic, so fluency at this very early age would have taken hold and be naturally acquired. Unfortunately, many parents say: " Oh, yes, my child understands Arabic but responds in English. He does not speak it well and is embarrassed to respond in the language of our heritage." Hence, the good old simple rule: "Practice makes perfect." Use it, practice it and apply it to yourself and to your child. Insist and persist until your child speaks back to you in your native tongue and do not worry about English. This will not diminish your child's competency in English, neither in fluency nor in accuracy.

About the Book

This book is a basic, direct and self-guided handbook to learn Levantine dialect. It is a simple, easy to use textbook for both the motivated student and teacher alike. It is useful for beginners with no knowledge of Arabic and for those who have had about a semester or two of either dialect or MSA. It is particularly helpful for people who are going to travel to the Levant for the first time or those who have lived there for a while and need to master and reinforce what they have learned.

I believe in circulating and recycling of vocabulary. This process helps in memorization, retention and visualization of words and short phrases. I also recommend that from day one, do not read silently, rather say each word out loud. There is a direct link between your mouth and your ear, and the benefit of hearing the music and enunciation of words contributes directly to retention and fluency as well as to overcoming your shyness or embarrassment when you interact with natives in the streets of any city in the Levant.

Since this is a dialect textbook and as such is geared towards oral fluency rather than written accuracy, towards communication rather than documentation, the amount of grammatical rules and explanations included here is limited to what is deemed necessary and immediate to facilitate fluency and aid in the communication process.

The focus here is on the delivery of a clear message and in obtaining a quick and valid response. Accuracy, and certainly fluency, are the product of practice, repetition and memorization. Study, review, memorize, say it out loud and keep testing yourself, alone or with a partner. You can do this. Do not get discouraged.

The book is designed for foreign students who have little or no knowledge of Arabic, formal or informal. It can be used by students themselves on their own, or with the help of an instructor or a tutor. Basically every word is introduced in three forms: Arabic form, transliteration form and English meaning. A beginner non-native who only desires to speak and communicate orally can rely on transliteration and English, while a more experienced student, a heritage student or a non-native with a year of exposure to Arabic who can read and has learned some basic survival vocabulary, may also benefit from the Arabic script and the grammatical notes available in the book.

Even if you are well versed in MSA, you still need to have this book. You may already be able to read the newspaper headlines or listen to the news and read a street sign, but it will sound very awkward to use MSA when you meet and greet someone, need a taxi, ask for directions, bargain and negotiate, open a bank account, order a meal or a sandwich, chat with someone in the street or in a café, enter a supermarket or a store, ask for the time, or make an appointment and get to know someone on a personal or even professional level, etc.

The book is divided into 72 sections, and 24 lessons, mainly by topic. Each section contains pertinent vocabulary needed and used when dealing with the situation at hand. So if you are looking for a word about clothing, or medicine, for example, you simply look in that particular section. There are also sufficient exercises in translation with answers provided for you to doublecheck and verify your knowledge. Do the exercise first before you look up the answer. Continuously test yourself, memorize new words, read and speak out loud even when you are alone and pick the brain of a native friend or acquaintance. Lebanese, and Arabs in general, are impressed when you attempt to speak Arabic with them. They will go out of their way to help you and make your acquaintance. However, they will also try first to practice their English or French with you. Most of them are bilingual or even trilingual. Do not fall for this. Insist on using your Arabic first.

The best way to learn a foreign language is through total immersion. Go ahead, immerse yourself. You will be forced to float. Drowning is not an option. You are too smart to drown. Study this book, and find a group of natives to chat with. Better yet, visit Lebanon and have some *maza*, *tabbouli* and *araq*. Then, we'll talk. Do not be afraid to make mistakes. Keep on trying. Practice makes perfect.

Best of luck. Welcome to the Levant and to Lebanon.

George Nicolas El-Hage, Ph.D.

1 - A Critical Reference Table to Visit Frequently

(Continued on the Next Page)

Non-Connector	Connector	Final Position	Medial Position	Initial position	Independent Position
X		ـا	ـا	ا	ا
	X	ـب	ـبـ	بـ	ب
	X	ـت	ـتـ	تـ	ت
	X	ـث	ـثـ	ثـ	ث
	X	ـج	ـجـ	جـ	ج
	X	ـح	ـحـ	حـ	ح
	X	ـخ	ـخـ	خـ	خ
X		ـد	ـد	د	د
X		ـذ	ـذ	ذ	ذ
X		ـر	ـر	ر	ر
X		ـز	ـز	ز	ز
	X	ـس	ـسـ	سـ	س
	X	ـش	ـشـ	شـ	ش
	X	ـص	ـصـ	صـ	ص
	X	ـض	ـضـ	ضـ	ض
	X	ـط	ـطـ	طـ	ط
	X	ـظ	ـظـ	ظـ	ظ
	X	ـع	ـعـ	عـ	ع
	X	ـغ	ـغـ	غـ	غ
	X	ـف	ـفـ	فـ	ف

	X	ـق	ـقـ	قـ	ق
	X	ـك	ـكـ	كـ	ك
	X	ـل	ـلـ	لـ	ل
	X	ـم	ـمـ	مـ	م
	X	ـن	ـنـ	نـ	ن
	X	ـه	ـهـ	هـ	ه
X		ـو	ـو	و	و
	X	ـي	ـيـ	يـ	ي

2 - The Arabic Alphabet: Includes 28 Letters:

ا ب ت ث ج ح خ د ذ ر ز س ش ص ض
ط ظ ع غ ف ق ك ل م ن ه و ي.
(لا) - (ء)

3 - The Alphabet: Grouped by family of seemingly similar letters in shape; the dots above or under the letter determine its name, sound and function:

	ا
	ب ت ث
	ج ح خ
	د ذ
	ر ز
	س ش
	ص ض
	ط ظ
	ع غ
	ف ق
	ك ل
	م ن ه و ي.

لا = this is called: Laam Alif – a letter composed of combining two letters: ل ا
ء = this is called Hamza. Its sound resembles the glottal stop in some English words like Adam, apple, inner, uncle. The Hamza can take different positions in a word with certain letters. It can also sit by itself. Examples: أ – إ – ؤ - ء – ئ ى

4 - Pronouncing the Alphabet Letters:

ا	=	Alif (as in apple)
ب	=	Ba (as in book)
ت	=	Ta (as in time)
ث	=	Tha (as in three)
ج	=	Jiim
ح	=	Ha (the heavy h)
خ	=	Kha
د	=	Daal (as in down)
ذ	=	Dhaal (as in The book)
ر	=	Ra (as in rookie)
ز	=	Zay (as in zebra)
س	=	siin (as in sun)
ش	=	Shiin (as in shut)
ص	= Saad (the heavy s) as in suddenly	
ض	= Dhaad (as in a heavy d)	
ط	=	Tah (as in a heavy t)
ظ	=	Zah (as in heavy The)
ع	= 'Ayn (as in deep a)	
غ	= Ghayn (as in a gargling sound)	
ف	= Fa (as in Fat)	
ق	= Qaaf (as in deep q)	
ك	= Kaaf (as in keep)	
ل	= Laam (as in lamb)	

م = Miim (as in mine)	
ن = Nuun (as in nine)	
ه = ha (as in hope)	
و = Waw (as in wow)	
ي = Ya (as in yahoo)	
لا = Laam Alif (as in la)	
ء = hamza	

5 – Again, Arabic letters in their three positions in a word: Initial, Medial, Final. The first letter from the right is the full size letter followed by: Initial, Medial, and Final positions. You can also refer to the earlier Chart Number 1.

Final Medial Initial

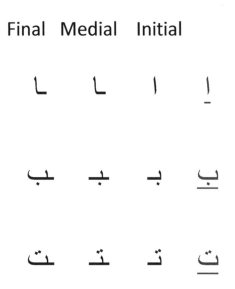

ث ثـ ثـ ثـ

ج جـ جـ جـ

ح حـ حـ حـ

خ خـ خـ خـ

د د د د

ذ ذ ذ ذ

ر ر ر ر

ز ز ز ز

س سـ سـ سـ

ش شـ شـ شـ

ص صـ ـصـ ـص

ض ضـ ـضـ ـض

ط طـ ـطـ ـط

ظ ظـ ـظـ ـظ

ع عـ ـعـ ـع

غ غـ ـغـ ـغ

ف فـ ـفـ ـف

ق قـ ـقـ ـق

ك كـ ـكـ ـك

ل لـ ـلـ ـل

م ‍ـم ‍مـ ‍م

ن ‍ـنـ ‍نـ ‍ن

ه ‍ـهـ ‍هـ ‍ة

و ‍ـو ‍و ‍و

ي ‍ـيـ ‍يـ ‍ي

6 - Connectors and Non-connectors

The Arabic Alphabet letters are of two kinds: Connectors and Non-connectors
The Connectors are those letters that connect with a letter that comes before or after them
The Non-connectors are those letters that connect with the letter that comes before them but not after them.

These are the Connectors:

ب ت ث
ج ح خ
س ش
ص ض
ط ظ
ع غ
ف ق
ك ل
م ن ه ي.

These are the Non-connectors:

ا د ذ ر ز و

Examples of letters that connect:

غيم	عنب	بيت	بنت

Examples of letters that do not connect:

مردود	رواد	غروب	عالم	ادرس

7 - Important Landmarks:

Madda: (~) sits over the Alif and prolongs its pronunciation.
Alif = A أ - ا but with the Madda over it, it reads AA = آ
Shadda: is like a small **w** = (ّ) sits over a letter and doubles its pronunciation so the letter is not written twice.
- أوّل - علّم - سلّم = Sallam - 'Allam - Awwal

Sukoun: is like a small circle (ْ) sits over the letter and silences its pronunciation.
بْ - سْ - ثْ = t – s – b –

Kasra: (ِ) sits under the letter and gives it the (e) sound.
لِ - قِ - بِ = be - qe - le

FatHa: (َ) sits above the letter and gives it the (A) like in French, sound.
سَ - وَ - بَ = ba - wa - sa

Damma: (ُ) sits over the letter and gives it the (u) sound.
رُ - لُ – بُ = bu – lu – ru

Tanween: is doubling the FatHa, Kasra, or Damma. It gives a letter the an/in/un/ sound.
مً - فً - بً = ban – fan - lan
Although the tanween FatHa usually sits on the alif
(ا) ماً - فاً - باً
لٍ – فٍ - بٍ = bin - fin - lin
لٌ – فٌ – بٌ = bun – fun -lun

8 - Short and Long Vowels:

Short Vowels:		
Damma ُ	FatHa َ	Kasra ِ
	be – ba - bu بِ بَ بُ	

Long Vowels:
ا - و - ي -
باب - نون - بيت
Baab - Noon - Bayyt

9 - The Importance of Dots and Vowels

Please pay attention. These words may look alike, but their meaning, dictated by different dots and vowels, is certainly different. Example:

قَبْل	qabl	before
قِيْل	qeel	was said
فِيْل	feel	elephant
قَتَلَ	qatala	he killed
قُتِلَ	qutila	was killed
بِنْت	bint	girl
نَبْت	nabt	plant
بَيْت	bayt	house

10 - Connecting Letters: Word Formation

Connecting letters: Word Formation			
اسم	ا س م	Ism	Name
اسمي	ا س م ي	ismi	My name is
طالب	ط ا ل ب	Taalib	student
مصر	م ص ر	miSr	Egypt
جامعة	ج ا م ع ة	jaami 'a	university
شارع	ش ا ر ع	shaari '	street
ادب	ا د ب	adab	literature
حلو	ح ل و	Hilou	sweet/beautiful
فرصة	ف ر ص ة	furSa	break
سوق	س و ق	souq	market
شتي	ش ت ي	shiti	rain/winter
موسم	م و س م	mawsim/faSl	season
لبنان	ل ب ن ا ن	lubnaan	Lebanon
آب	آ ب	aab	august
تمّوز	ت م م و ز	tammouz	july
بيروت	ب ي ر و ت	Bayrout	Beirut

Word meaning and transliteration in the order of the words above:
Name = ism // my name (is) = ismi // student = Taalib // Egypt = MiSr // university = jaami 'a // street = shaari ' // literature = adab // beautiful or sweet = Hilou // break or vacation = furSa // market = souq // rain/winter = shiti// season = mawsim/faSl // Lebanon = Lubnaan // August = aab // July = tammouz // Beirut = Bayrout

11 – The Definite Article

The Definite Article:
The = ال = al
بيت = البيت Bayt = al bayt = house - the house

12 - The Adjective

The adjective follows the gender of the noun it describes. If the noun is masculine, the adjective is masculine. If the noun is feminine, then the adjective is feminine:		
Walad Taweel (m.)	a tall boy	ولد طويل
Bint Taweeli (f.)	a tall girl	بنت طويلة

13 - Pronunciation Legend:

Symbol Letter	Pronunciation
Ḍ ḍ dh ض	Dhad
Ḥ ḥ H ح	Ha
Ṣ ṣ S ص	Sad
Ṭ ṭ T ط	Ta
ʿa, ʿu, ʿi , ʿ ع	ayn
ʾa, ʾu, ʾi أ	alif
ā or aa آ	aa
ū or (oo) or (ou) و	wow
ī or (ii) or (ee) ي	yaa
MS =	masculine singular
FS =	Feminine singular

Critical Vocabulary for Certain Situations and Topics (At A Glance)

14 - The Four Seasons

The Four Seasons - al fuSoul al arba 'a		الفصول الأربعة
al Sayf	Summer	الصيف
al khareef	Fall	الخريف
al shiti	Winter	الشتي
al rabii '	Spring	الربيع

15 - The Four Directions

The Four Directions: al ittijaahat al arba 'a		الاتجاهات الأربعة
al sharq	East	الشرق
al gharb	West	الغرب
al shamaal	North	الشمال
al janub	South	الجنوب

16 - Greetings and Such

Greetings and Such		تحيّات
taHiyyaat	تحيّات	Greetings:
marHaba	hello	مرحبا
ahla w sahla	welcome	أهلا وسهلاً

kiifak ilyawm?	how are you today (MS)	كيفَك اليوم
kiifik ilyawm?	how are you today (FS)	كيفِك اليوم
alsalaamu 'alaykum	peace be upon you	السلام عليكم
wa 'alaykum al salaam	and peace upon you (reply)	وعليكم السلام
tsharrafna	honored to meet you	تشرفنا
sabaH al khayr	good morning	صباح الخير
sabaH al nour	good morning (reply)	صباح النور
masa al khayr	good evening	مسا الخير
masa al noor	good evening (reply)	مسا النور
min fadhlak	please (MS)	من فضلَك
min fadhlik	please (FS)	من فضلك
shoukran	thank you	شكراً
'afwan	you are welcome/ excuse me	عفواً
mitassif	sorry	متأسف
kiif?	how?	كيف
laysh?	why?	ليش
shou?	what?	شو
shou fii?	what's going on?	شو في
miin?	who?	مين
wayn?	where?	وين
min wayn?	from where?	مِن وين
amtiin?	when?	امتين
inshallah	God willing	انشالله
iza Alla raad	if God willed so	إزا الله ر اد
ma ' al salaami	goodbye	مع السلامة
min	from	مِن
Ma '	with	مع
'ala	on	على
maa fi	there isn't	ما في
maa fi mashkale	there is no problem	ما في مشكلة
bshoufak bukra	see you (MS) tomorrow	بشوفك بكرا

ba 'daan	later on	بعدان
bukra	tomorrow	بكرا
al yawm	today	اليوم
mbaariH	yesterday	مبارح
ams	yesterday	أمس
'azizi	my dear (MS)	عزيزي
'azizati	my dear (FS)	عزيزتي
taHiyyaati	my Greetings	تحياتي
salaam	hello – peace	سلام
salaamaat	Greetings	سلامات
iHtiraam	respect	احترام

17 - Holidays

a 'yaad	Holidays	أعياد
'iid sa 'iid	happy holiday	عيد سعيد
'iid mbaarak	blessed holiday	عيد مبارك
'iid raas al sini	New Year's Eve	عيد راس السنة
'iid al mawlid al nabawi	Birth of the Prophet	عيد المولد النبوي
'iid al miilaad	Christmas	عيد الميلاد
'iid al fiSSH	Easter	عيد الفصح
'iid al kabiir	Easter	عيد الكبير
ramaDhaan kariim	happy Ramadan	رمضان كريم
hadaaya	gifts	هدايا
Hidiye	gift	هديي
sha ' nini	Palm Sunday	شعنيني
iddees	saint	قديس
Kneesee	church	كنيسة
jaami '	mosque	جامع
shaykh	sheik	شيخ
Khoury	priest	خوري
muTraan	bishop	مطران
mufti	grand sheik	مفتي

baTrak	patriarch	بطرك
al baaba	the Pope	البابا
masjid	mosque	مسجد
al qur'aan al kariim	Holy Koran	القرآن الكريم
al kitaab al muqaddas	Holy book	الكتاب المقدّس
al injeel	the Bible	الانجيل
qurbaan	holy bread/ host	قربان
bakhour	incense	بخور
mabkhara	incense burner	مبخرة
masbaHa	prayer beads/worry beads	مسبحة
madbaH	alter	مدبح
wudhu'	ablution	وضوء
'imaadi	baptism	عمادة
zawaaj madani	civil marriage	زواج مدني
' urs	wedding	عرس
' arees	groom	عريس
' arus	bride	عروس
Ishbeen	best man	اشبين
' aqd zawaaj	marriage contract	عقد زواج
Talaaq	divorce	طلاق
shahr al 'asal	honey moon	شهر العسل
Habal	pregnancy	حبل
awlaad	children	اولاد
i 'tiraaf	confession	اعتراف
munaawali	communion	مناولة
Salaa	prayer	صلاة
Salla	to pray	صلّى
Haflit isti'baal	reception party	حفلة استقبال
fustaan al 'urs	wedding dress	فستان العرس

18 – Niceties and Questions

Niceties and Qquestions	mujaamalaat w as'ili	مجاملات وأسئلة
juwwa	inside	جوا
barra	outside	برا
fawq/faw'	above, over	فوق
taHt	under, below	تحت
ma ' miin?	with whom	مع مين
shou Saar?	what happened	شو صار
tikhmiin	perhaps	تخمين
walaw!	Is that so	ولو
hayk?	Is that so?	هيك
mish ma 'qul	impossible	مش معقول
shou awlak?	What do you say (MS)?	شو قولَك
shou awlik?	What do you say (FS)?	شو قولِك
shou aal?	What did he say?	شو قال
shou aalit?	What did she say?	شو قالت
ma smi 't	I did not hear	ما سمعت
ma fhimt	I did not understand	ما فهمت
fhimnaa	we understood	فهمنا
mafhoom?	Is this understood?	مفهوم
mumtaaz	perfect	ممتاز
'aziim	great	عزيم
ktiir mniiH	very good	كتير منيح
'ala kil Haal	any how	على كل حال
ma twakhizni	forgive me	ما تواخزني
saamiHni	forgive me	سامحني
ma tloomni	do not blame me	ما تلومني
bi 'tizir	I apologize	بعتزر
alla ma 'ak	May God be with you (MS)	الله معك
alla ma 'ik	May God be with you (FS)	الله معِك
ya laTiif	this is something	يا لطيف
mamnoon	I am grateful	ممنون
ya salaam	wow	يا سلام

19 - The Weather

The weather can be:		الطقس
al Taqs/ alTa's	weather	الطقس
al Jaw	weather	الجو
al manaakh	climate	المناخ
Hilou	beautiful	حلو
baarid	cold	بارد
Mu 'tadil	moderate	معتدل
mumTir	rainy	ممطر
daafii	warm	دافي
mushmis	sunny	مشمس
ghaa'im	cloudy	غائم
SaaHi	dry	صاحي
muthlij	snowy	مثلج
'aaSif	stormy	عاصف
hawa	air	هوا
reeH	wind	ريح
'aaSfi	storm	عاصفة
baHr	sea	بحر
al baHr	the sea	البحر
haa'ij	wavy, stormy	هائج
mawj	waves	موج
madd	flow	مدّ
jazr	ebb	جزر
raml	sand	رمل
shaT	shore	شط
nahr	river	نهر
buHayra	lake	بحيرة

nab '	fountain	نبع
Tabi 'a	nature	طبيعة
ghaym	clouds	غيم
samaa	sky	سما
ardh	earth/land	أرض
qamar/ amar	moon	قمر
shams	sun	شمس
njoum	stars	نجوم
hawa	air	هوا
traab	earth/dust	تراب
waHl	mud	وحل
dhabaab	fog	ضباب
zilzaal	earthquake	زلزال
i 'Saar	tornado	إعصار
kawkab	planet	كوكب
bar'/barq	lightening	برق
ra 'd	thunder	رعد
mawjit Harr	heat wave	موجة حر
rToubi	humidity	رطوبة
zilzaal	earthquake	زلزال

20 - Days of the Week & Time

Days of the Week:	ayyaam al usbu '	أيام الأسبوع
al aHad – al tanayn - al talaata - al arba 'a - al khamiis - al jum 'a - al sabt –		
Sunday – Monday – Tuesday - Wednesday - Thursday - Friday - Saturday		
		الأحد ـ الاثنين ـ التلاتا ـ الأربعا – الخميس ـ الجمعة ـ السبت

yawm	day	يوم
ayyaam	days	أيام
shahr	month	شهر
ashhur - shuhur	months	أشهر – شهور
sana/sini	year	سنة
sanawaat - siniin	years	سنوات
saa 'a	hour	ساعة
saa 'aat	hours	ساعات
daqiqa	minute	دقيقة
daqaa'iq	minutes	دقائق
laHza	second	لحظة
laHazaat	seconds	لحظات
sanawaat - siniin	years	سنوات
nahaar	day time	نهار
layl	night	ليل
usbou '	week	اسبوع
jim 'a	week	جمعة
saa 'a	hour	ساعة
niS saa 'a	half hour	نص ساعة
rub ' saa 'a	quarter of an hour	ربع ساعة
tilt saa 'a	twenty minutes	تلت ساعة
al SubH	morning	الصبح
al dhuhr	noon	الضهر

al masa	evening	المسا
'ashiyi	evening	عشيي
ba 'd al dhuhr	afternoon	بعد الضهر
abl al dhuhr	before noon	قبل الضهر
iddaysh al saa 'a	what time is it?	قديش الساعة
shu al saa 'a	what time is it?	شو الساعة
Halaq/hala'	now	هلّق
al waqt/al wa't	time	الوقت
al ghuroub	sunset	الغروب
al fajr	dawn	الفجر
niS saa 'a	half hour	نص ساعة
rub ' saa 'a	quarter of an hour	ربع ساعة
'ashiyi	evening	عشيي

21- The Twelve Months of the Year

The Twelve Months of the Year:	شهور السنة	shuhur l sini
kaanun al taani	January	كانون التاني
shubaaT	February	شباط
aadaar	March	آدار
nisaan	April	نيسان
ayyaar	May	أيار
Huzayraan	June	حزيران
tammouz	July	تمّوز
aab	August	آب
ayloul	September	ايلول
tishriin al awwal	October	تشرين الأول
tishriin al taani	November	تشرين التاني
kaanun al awwal	December	كانون الأول

22 - Family Members and Relatives

Family members and relatives:		أفراد العيلة والقرايب
Afraad l 'ayli wil araayib		
fard	member	فرد
afraad	members	افراد
'ayli	family	عيلي
araayib	relatives	ارايب
bayy - abb - waaled	father	بي - أب - والد -
imm – waaldeh	mother	ام - والدة -
khay - akh - shaqiiq	brother	خي – أخ - شقيق -
ikht - shaqiqa	sister	اخت ـ شقيقة
'amm	paternal uncle	عمّ
khaal	maternal uncle	خال
'amma	paternal aunt	عمّة
khala	maternal aunt	خالة
jadd – Jidd	grandfather	جدّ
Jadda – Sittu	grandmother	جدّة ـ ستو
ibn	son (of)	ابن
ibn 'amm	paternal cousin. Male.	ابن عمّ
bint 'amm	paternal cousin. Female	بنت عم
bint	daughter (of)	بنت
Sihr	brother- in- law	صهر
Hamaat	mother- in- law	حماة
' amm	father- in- law	عمّ
mara	woman	مرا
rijjaal	man	رجال

45

marti	my wife	مرتي
Jawzi	my husband	جوزي
mjawwaz	married	مجوّز
a 'zab	single	أعزب
mTallaq	divorced	مطلّق
khaaTib	engaged	خاطب
khaTeebee	fiancé	خطيبة
armal	widow (MS)	أرمل
armali	widow (FS)	ارملة
yateem	orphan	يتيم
shabb	young man	شبّ
Sabiyyee	young woman	صبيّة
khityaar	old man	ختيار
khityaara	old woman	ختيارة
'ajouz	old person	عجوز
shboubiyye	good looking	شبوبية
mshabshib	looking younger	مشبشب

23 – The Numbers

al a 'daad	
The Numbers:	الأعداد
waaHad - itnayn - tlaati - arb 'a – khamsi - sitti - sab 'a - tmaany - tis 'a - 'ashra – Sifr –	
	0 - 10 - 9 – 8 – 7 – 6 – 5 – 4 – 3 – 2 – 1
'ashra – 'ishreen - tlaatiin – arb 'iin - khamsiin - sittiin - sab 'iin - tmaaniin - tis 'iin - miyyi –	
	- 100 - 90 - 80 - 70 - 60 - 50 - 40 - 30 - 20 – 10
miyyi = 100 //// 'ashra = 10 /// alf = 1000 /// malyoon = 1000 000	
iHda 'sh – itna 'sh – talata 'sh – arba 'ta 'sh – khamista 'sh – sitta 'sh – sabata 'sh – tamanta 'sh – tis 'ta 'sh – 'ishriin –	
	– 20 – 19 – 18 – 17 – 16 – 15 - 14 – 13 – 12 – 11
'ishreen - 20 = عشرين	
waaHad w 'ishriin =	21	واحد وعشرين
itnayn w 'ishriin =	22	تنين وعشرين
tlata w 'ishriin =	23	تلاتة وعشرين
arba 'a w 'ishriin =	24	اربعة وعشرين
khamsa w 'ishriin =	25	خمسة وعشرين
sitta w 'ishriin =	26	ستة وعشرين
sab 'a w 'ishriin =	27	سبعة وعشرين
tmaany w 'ishriin =	28	تماني وعشرين
tis 'a w 'ishriin =	29	تسعة وعشرين
tlaatiin =	30	تلاتين

24 - Some Useful Verbs

Some useful verbs:		أفعال مفيدة
af 'aal mufeedi		
daras =	(he) studied	درس
katab =	wrote	كتب
naam =	slept	نام
raaH =	went	راح
ijaa =	came	إجا
li 'ib =	played	لعب
harab =	escaped	هرب
akal =	ate	أكل
dakhal =	entered	دخل
kharaj =	exited	خرج
qara' =	read	قرأ
fataH =	opened	فتح
rasam =	drew	رسم
simi ' =	heard	سمع
shirib =	drank	شرب
fihim =	understood	فهم
sa'al =	asked	سأل
sakan =	resided	سكن
'imil =	did	عمل
tarjam =	translated	ترجم
Wi 'i =	woke up	وعي
nisi =	forgot	نسي
fakkar	thought	فكّر
libis	dressed	لبس
shalaH	undressed	شلح
jaayyee	coming	جايي
raayeH	going	رايح
kaan	was	كان
kaanit (FS)	she was	كانت
shaaf	he saw	شاف

shaafit	she saw	شافت
sakkar	he closed	سَكَّر
sakkarit	she closed	سكّرت

The majority of these verbs are in the (M.S) form. To form the (F.S.), simply add a ت (-it) to the end of each verb:		
daras =	he studied	درس
darasit =	she studied	درس + ت = درست
katab =	he wrote	كتب
katabit =	she wrote	كتب + ت = كتبت
naam =	he slept	نام
naamit =	she slept	نام + ت = نامت

25 – "I want to"...plus a Verb

I want to...	ana baddi...	انا بدّي
rouH	go	روح
ijee	come	إجي
zour	visit	زور
aakul	eat	آكل
ishrab	drink	إشرب
naam	sleep	نام
a 'rif	know	أعرف
ishtiri	buy	اشتري
bii '	sell	بيع
uTlub	request	اطلب
ista'jir	rent	استأجر
irkab	ride	اركب
irja '	return	إرجع
i'ra/ iqra	read	إقرا
i 'zum	invite	اعزم
iftaH	open	افتح
sakkir	close	سكّر
Isma '	listen	اسمع
It 'asha	eat dinner	اتعشى

26 - Frequently Asked Questions

Frequently Asked Questions:		اسئلة دايمن منسألها
shou ismak?	What is your name?	شو اسمك؟
min wayn int?	Where are you from?	من وين انت؟
shou bta 'mil?	What do you do	شو بتعمل؟
shou btishtighil?	What do you do?	شو بتشتغل؟
wayn raayeH?	Where are you going?	وين رايح؟
wayn kint?	Where were you?	وين كنت؟
shou fi jdeed?	What is new?	شو في جديد؟
shou ma 'ak?	What do you have?	شو معك؟
laysh t'akhart?	Why are you late?	ليش تأخرت؟
shou bitHib taakul?	What do you like to eat?	شو بتحب تاكل
shou bitHib tishrab?	What do you like to drink?	شو بتحب تشرب؟
keef bitHib al ahwi?	How do you like the coffee?	كيف بتحب القهوي؟
mjawwaz aw a 'zab?	Are you married or single?	مجوز او أعزب؟
shou 'indak wlaad?	How many children do you have?	شو عندك ولاد؟
wayn saakin?	Where do you live?	وين ساكن؟
ma ' meen saakin?	Whom do you live with?	مع مين ساكن؟
keef jeet?	How did you come?	كيف جيت؟
shu arrart ta 'mil?	What did you decide to do?	شو قررت تعمل؟
shu ma 'ak maSary?	How much money do you have?	شو معك مصاري؟
ibn meen int?	Whose son are you?	ابن مين انت؟

27 - The Pronouns

The Pronouns: aldhamaa'r		الضمائر
ana =	I – I am	انا
inta =	You M.S.	انتَ
intii =	You F.S.	انتِ
intu =	You two M. or F	انتو
huwwi =	He – He is	هوي
hiyyi =	She – She is	هيي
hinni =	They M. or F	هني
niHna =	We – Us M. or F.	نحن
intu =	You plural. M. or F.	انتو

28 - The Possessive Pronouns

The Possessive Pronouns: using the word ktaab = book				
ضمائر الملكيّة using the word: book				
my book – your book – etc.				
ana =	I – I am	انا	ktaab(i)	كتابي
inta =	You M.S	انتَ	ktaab(ak)	كتابَك
intii =	You F.S	انتِ	ktaab(ik)	كتابِك
intu =	You two M	انتو	ktaab(kun)	كتابكن
huwwi =	He – He is	هوي	ktab(u)	كتابو
hiyyi =	She – She is	هيي	ktaab(a)	كتابا
hinni =	They M or	هني	ktaab(un)	كتابن
nihna =	We – Us M or F	نحن	ktaab(na)	كتابنا

intu =	You plural M or F انتو	ktaab(kun)	كتابكن

more examples with: bayt – ism – ma ' = house – name – with-			
my house – your house – etc			
my name – your name – etc			
with me – with you - etc			
bayti	ismi	ma 'i	بيتي – اسمي – معي -
Baytak	ismak	ma 'ak	بيتَك ـ اسمَك ـ معَك -
Baytik	ismik	ma 'ik	بيتِك – اسمِك – معِك -
Baytkun	ismkun	ma 'kun	بيتكن – اسمكن – معكن -
Baytu	ismu	ma 'u	بيتو – اسمو – معو -
Bayta	isma	ma 'a	بيتا – اسما – معا -
Baytna	ismna	ma 'na	بيتنا ـ اسمنا ـ معنا -
Baytkun	ismkun	ma 'kun	بيتكن – اسمكن – معكن -

29 – Sample Conjugations

Sample Conjugations:				
baddi – I want (to) بدّي				
ana	I – I am	انا	baddi	بدّي
inta =	You M.S.	انتَ	baddak	بدَّك
intii =	You F.S.	انتِ	baddik	بدِّك
intu =	You two	انتو	badkun	بدكن
huwwi =	He – He is	هوي	baddu	بدّو
hiyyi =	She – She is	هيي	badda	بدا
hinni =	They M. or F	هني	baddun	بدن
nihna =	We – Us M. or F.	نحن	badna	بدنا
intu =	You plural. M. or F.	انتو	badkun	بدكن

ana baddi ishrab =	**I want to drink**		انا بدّي اشرب
ana	I – I am	انا	baddi ishrab (I)
inta	You M.S.	انتَ	baddak tishrab (T-I)
intii	You F.S.	انتِ	baddik tishrabi (T-I)
intu	You two M or F	انتو	badkun tishrabu (T-U)
huwwi	He – He is	هوي	baddu yishrab (Y)
hiyyi	She – She is	هيي	badda tishrab (T)
hinni	They M or F	هني	baddun yishrabu(Y-U)
nihna	We – Us M. or F.	نحن	badna nishrab (N)
intu	You plural. M. or F	انتو	badkun tishrabu (T- U)

ana baddi naam =		I want to sleep	أنا بدّي نام
ana =	I – I a	انا	baddi naam
inta =	You MS	انتَ	baddak tnaam (T)
intii =	You FS	انتِ	baddik tnaami (T-I)
intu =	You two	انتو	badkun tnaamu (T-U)
huwwi =	He – He is	هوي	baddu ynaam (Y)
hiyyi =	She – She is	هيي	badda tnaam (T)
hinni =	They M or F	هني	baddun ynaamu(Y-U)
nihna =	We – Us M or F نحن		badna nnaam (N)
intu =	You plural M or F انتو		badkun tnaamu (T- U)

ana baddi idrus / ishrab/ iktub	ادرس – اشرب – اكتب -
inta baddak tidrus/ tishrab/ tiktub	تدرس- تشرب – تكتب -
inti baddik tidirsi/ tishrabi/ tikitbi	تدرسي – تشربي - تكتبي -
intu badkun tidirsu/ tishrabu tikitbu	تدرسو – تشربو – تكتبو
huwi baddu yidrus/ yishrab/ yiktub	يدرس – يشرب – يكتب
hiyyi badda tidrus/ tishrab/ tiktub	تدرس – تشرب – تكتب
hinni baddun yidirsu/ yishrabu/ yikitbu	يدرسو –يشربو – يكتبو
niHna badna nidrus/ nishrab/ niktub	ندرس – نشرب – نكتب
intu badkun tidirsu/ tishrabu/ tikitbu	تدرسو –تشربو – تكتبو

I am drinking now: present continuous		
ana =	I – I am	انا ' am ishrab (I)
inta =	You M.S.	انتَ ' am tishrab (T)
intii =	You F.S.	انتِ ' am tishrabi (T-I)
intu =	You two M. or F	انتو ' am tishrabu (T-U)

huwwi = He – He is	هوي	' am yishrab (Y)	
hiyyi = She – She is	هيي	' am tishrab (T)	
hinni = They M. or F	هني	' am yishrabu(Y-U)	
nihna = We – Us M. or F.	نحن	' am nishrab (N)	
intu = You plural. M. or F.	انتو	' am tishrabu (T-U)	

I drank. Past tense(shribt)			
ana = I – I am	انا	shribt	انا شربتْ
inta = You MS	انتَ	shrib	انتَ شربتْ
intii = You FS	انتِ	shribti	انتِ شربتِ
intu = You two M or F	انتو	shribtu	انتو شربتو
huwwi =He – He is	هوي	shirib	هوي شِربْ
hiyyi = She – She is	هيي	shirbit	هيي شِربتْ
hinni = They M or F	هني	shirbu	هني شربو
nihna = We M or F	نحن	shribna	نحن شربنا
intu = You plural M or F	انتو	shribtu	انتو شربتو

30 - Kaan - was - Past Tense

Kaan - was - past tense –	كان		
ana = I – I am	انا	kint	انا كنتْ
inta = You M.S.	انتَ	kint	انتَ كنتْ
intii = You F.S.	انتِ	kinti	انتِ كنتِ
intu = You two M. or F	انتو	kintu	انتو كنتو
huwwi He – He is	هوي	kaan	هوي كان
hiyyi = She – She is	هيي	kaanit	هيي كانتْ
hinni = They M. or F	هني	kaanu	هني كانو
nihna = We – Us M	نحن	kinna	نحن كنا
intu = You plural. M. or F.	انتو	kintu	انتو كنتو
Ana kint ' am baakul = I was eating –			انا كنت عم باكل

31- More Conjugations in the Past Tense

More Conjugations in the past tense: daras – naam – saafar		
Studied – slept – travelled -		
ana = I – I am	انا	darast/// nimt/// saafart
inta = You M.S.	انتَ	darast/// nimt/// saafart
intii = You F.S.	انتِ	darasti/// nimti/// saafarti
intu = You two M. or F	انتو	darastu /// nimtu///saafartu
huwwi He – He is	هوي	daras/// naam/// saafar
hiyyi = She – She is	هي	darasit/// naamit///saafarit
hinni = They M. or F	هني	darasu ///naamu/// saafaru
nihna = We – Us M. or F	نحن	darasna/// nimnaa/// saafarna
intu = You plural M or F	انتو	darastu/// nimtu/// saafartu

ana baddi aakul	ana ' am baakul	Ana akalt
انا بدّي آكل	أنا عم باكل	انا أكلتْ
I want to eat	I am eating	I ate

32 - Negation

Negation:
ana ma akalt/ ana ma ' am baakul/ ana mish ' am baakul/ ana ma baddi aakul
(ma) and (mish) are used for negation: - مش - ما
ana darast --- ana ma darast
ana 'am bidrus --- ana ma 'ambidrus --- ana mish 'ambidrus –
I am studying – I am not studying – I am not studying -
huwi hawn --- huwi mish hawn   هوي هون--- هوي مش هون
huwi naam - huwi ma naam   هوي نام --- هوي ما نام

33- Qaaf & Hamza

The qaaf (ق) and the hamza(ء)
In many words the ق is softened to pronounce as the glottal ء = a:
fawq = faw' above
Qamar = amar moon
qaSd = aSd intention
you will get used to seeing both options throughout the book.

34 - Important Connectors

Important connectors	
' an = about = khabberni ' an al Haadis	عن
min = from = ijaa min al bayt	مِن
maa = negates the present and past = maa ' am baakul - ma akalt - ma baddi aakul	ما
mish = negates the noun and present continuous = mish hawn – mish Hilou – mish 'am baakul- mish huwwi	مش
b = in/at = bil bayt – bil siyyara – bil Sayf in the house – in the car – in the summer	ب
ma ' = with = ma 'i – ma 'na – ahwi ma ' sukkar	مع
bidoun = without = ahwi bidoun sukkar	بدون
bala = without = ahwi bala sukkar	بلا
' al = to the = raaH ' al bayt – ijaa ' al maktab	عل
' al = on/at = liktaab ' al Tawlee	عل
kaan = was (MS) = kaan bil ijtimaa ' – kaan hawn	كان
kaanit = was (FS) = kaanit bil bayt- kaanit hawneek	كانت
kaan fi = there was = kaan fi shiti – kaan fi bard	كان في
lil = for the = baddi Taabi ' lil maktoub - baddi fustaan lil ' urs	لل
Hatta = until – so that – baddi idrus Hatta injaH –	حتى
bass = but – huwi suree bass immu libnaaniyyi	بس

35- (Is) Always Implied

The (is) in verb to be is always implied:	
alkalb barra = the dog is outside	الكلب برا
huwwi 'am yaakul = he is eating	هوي عم ياكل
fee ijtimaa ' = there is a meeting	في اجتماع

36 - Comparative

Comparative and Superlative				
Taweel	aTwal (min)	tall	taller than	طويل اطول من
Sghiir	aSghar (min)	small	smaller than	صغير اصغر من
qaSeer	aqSar (min)	shor t	shorter than	قصير اقصر من
rafi '	arfa ' (min)	thin	thinner than	رفيع ارفع من
jameel	ajmal (min)	beautiful	more beautiful than	جميل اجمل من
nasheeT	anshaT (min)	energetic	more energetic than	نشيط انشط من

37- Where Are You From?

min wayn inta?	Where are you from?	من وين انتَ
ana min libnaan = ana libnaani (MS)	Lebanese	لبناني
ana min libnaan = ana libnaaniyye (FS)	Lebanese	لبنانيي
ana souree -	ana souriyye	Syrian	سوري
ana urduni –	ana urduniyyee	Jordanian	اردني
ana ' iraaqi –	ana ' iraaqiyyi	Iraqi	عراقي
ana sa 'udi –	ana sa 'udiyyi	Saudi	سعودي
ana masri –	ana masriyee	Egyptian	مصري
ana amercaani –	ana amercaniyye	American	امركاني
ana mish min hawn – I am not from here –		انا مش من هون
ana ajnabi –	I am a foreigner – (MS)	انا اجنبي
ana ghareeb –	I am a stranger –	انا غريب
ana ajnabiyyee	I am a foreigner (FS)	انا اجنبية

38 - The Colors

the colors:	alwaan	الوان	
M	F	P	
aHmar احمر	Hamra	Humr	Red
abyadh ابيض	baydha	beedh	white
azraq ازرق	zarqa	zirq	blue
akhdhar اخضر	khadra	khudhr	green
asmar اسمر	samra	sumr	tan
aSfar اصفر	Safra	Sufr	yellow
Aswad اسود	sawda	sood	black
ashqar اشقر	shaqra	shuqr	blond
binni بني	binniyyi	binni	brown
laymouni ليموني	laymouni	laymouni	orange
zahr زهر	zahr	zahr	pink
rmaadi رمادي	rmaadi	rmaadi	grey
faatiH فاتح	faatiH	faatiH	light
ghaamiq غامق	ghaamiq	ghaamiq	dark

39 - Descriptions

SifaaT	descriptions	صفات
Tawiil	tall	طويل
aSeer	short	قصير
rafii '	thin	رفيع
tkheen	thick	تخين
khafiif	light	خفيف
tqeel	heavy	تقيل
awee	strong	اوي (قوي)
dh 'eef	weak	ضعيف
mareedh	sick	مريض
dhayyiq	tight	ضيّق
waasi '	wide	واسع
fayyish	shallow	فيّش
ghamiiq	deep	غميق
kbeer	big	كبير
Sghiir	small	صغير
'atii'	old	عتيق
adeem	ancient	اديم (قديم)
Jdiid	new	جديد
Bishi '	ugly	بشع
Hilou	beautiful	حلو
mahdhoum	cute	مهضوم

'aali	high	عالي
ghaali	expensive	غالي
rikhiiS	cheap	رخيص
waaTi	low	واطي
mwassakh	dirty	موسّخ
indhiif	clean	نضيف
ghareeb	strange	غريب
mumkin	possible	ممكن
mish mumkin	impossible	مش ممكن
mustaHiil	impossible	مستحيل
mamnoo '	forbidden	ممنوع
marghoob	desired	مرغوب
majnoon	crazy	مجنون
'ajeeb	strange	عجيب
aTrash	deaf	اطرش
akhras	mute	اخرس
a 'ma	blind	اعمى
asla '	bold	أصلع
akhwat	crazy	اخوت
mahboul	stupid	مهبول
majnoon	mad	مجنون
kareem	generous	كريم
bakheel	miserly	بخيل
mumil	boring	ممل
mukhlis	sincere	مخلص
'adou	enemy	عدو
Sadeeq	friendly	صديق

nasheeT	energetic	نشيط
khajoul	shy	خجول
mhadhab	polite	مهذب
khaayif	afraid	خايف
wiqiH	aggressive	وقح
'aSabi	nervous	عصبي
abadhaay	strong/brave	قبضاي

40 - I could be...

I could be:		انا ممكن كون ana mumkin koon
ana	I – I am	أنا
ta 'baan	tired	تعبان
mirtaaH	rested	مرتاح
'aTshaan	thirsty	عطشان
jaw 'aan	hungry	جوعان
shab 'aan	full	شبعان
bardaan	cold	بردان
farHaan	happy	فرحان
za 'laan	sad	زعلان
kaslaan	lazy	كسلان
ghadhbaan	angry	غضبان
mashgoul	busy	مشغول
mawjood	available	موجود
Haadhir	ready	حاضر
shaaTir	clever	شاطر
zaki	smart	زكي
'abqari	genius	عبقري
Hmaar	donkey	حمار

41 - Countries and Capitals

bildaan w ' awaaSim countries and capitals			بلدان وعواصم
Balad	country		بلد
bildaan	countries		بلدان
Country	Capital	Capital/Country	Capital/Country
lubnaan	Beirut	لبنان بيروت	Beirut, Lebanon
suria	dimashq	سوريا – دمشق	Damascus,Syria
miSr	al qaahira	مصر – القاهرة	Cairo,Egypt
al 'iraaq	baghdad	العراق – بغداد	Baghdad,Iraq
al yaman	San 'a	اليمن – صنعاء	Sana,Yemen
alsa 'udia	alriyaadh	السعودية – الرياض	Riyadh,Saudi Arabia
al sudaan	al Khartoum	السودان – الخرطوم	Khartoum,Sudan
al maghrib	al rabaaT	المغرب – الرباط	Rabat, Morocco
tounis	tounis	تونس – تونس	Tunis, Tunisia
al urdun	' ammaan	الأردن – عمّان	Amman,Jordan
al imaarat al 'arabiyya al muttaHida United Arab Emirates abu dhabi الامارات العربية المتحدة – ابو ظبي			AbuDhabi, UAE
fransa	baarees	فرنسا – باريس	Paris,France
briTaania	London	بريطانيا – لندن	London, England
iiTaalia	roma	ايطاليا – روما	Rome,Italy
Ispania	madreed	اسبانيا – مدريد	Madrid, Spain
Rusiyya	moscow	روسيا – موسكو	Moscow,Russia
tirkiyya	anqara	تركيا – انقرة	Ankara,Turkey

42- More Useful Expressions

More useful expressions: ‘ibaaraat mufeedi		عبارات مفيدة
marhaba	Hello	مرحبا
kiifik	How are you? F. S.	كيفِك
kiifkun	How are you? P. M. or F.	كيفكن
ahla w sahla	Welcome	أهلا وسهلا
ilHamdilla	Thank God	الحمدلله
miin inta?	Who are you? M.S.	مين انتَ
miin inti?	Who are you? F.S	مين انتِ .
Hadhrit politely refers to a person instead of Inta/Inti		حضرة
miin Hadhirtak? Who are you? M.S. (politely asked)		مين حضرتَك
miin Hadhirtik? Who are you? F.S. (politely asked)		مين حضرتِك
min wayn Hadhirtak? Where are you from? (politely asked) وين حضرتك		مِن
Min wayn inta? Where are you from? (not as polite)		مِن وين انتَ
ismi …	My name is	إسمي
shu ism Hadhirtak? What is your name? (politely asked) حضرتَك		شو اسم
shu hayda?	What is this? M.S.	شو هيدا
shu haydi?	What is this? F.S.	شو هيدي
SabaaH ilKhayr	Good morning	صباح الخير
masa il Khayr	Good evening	مسا الخير
shukran	Thanks	شكراً
ma ‘ al salaami	Good bye	مع السلامة
min fadhlak	Please. M.S.	مِن فضلَك
Min fadhlik	Please. F.S	مِن فضلِك

wayn kint?	Where were you? M.S.	وين كنتْ
wayn kinti?	Where were you? F.S.	وين كنتِ
tasharrafna	Honored to meet you	تشرفنا
khalleek hawn	stay here	خليك هون
bshoufak	I'll see you	بشوفك
bshoufak bukra	see you tomorrow	بشوفك بكرا
jaayee	coming	جايي
raayeH	going	رايح
ijaa	he came	إجا
raaH	he went	راح
Talle	he showed up	طلّ
kaan	was	كان
kaan fi	there was	كان في
ma kaan fi	there wasn't	ما كان في
ni 'saan	sleepy	نعسان
ma tihtam	do not pay attention	ما تهتم
ana mish mihtam	I do not care	انا مش مهتم
Tawwil baalak	be patient (MS)	طوّل بالك
Tawlee baalik	be patient (FS)	طولي بالك
rouq/ rou'	calm down (MS)	روق
rouqi/rou'I	calm down(FS)	روقي
shou baddak minni	what do you want from me	شو بدّك مني
mish ' aayzak	I do not need you	مش عايزك
ma ' indi mazaaj	I am not in the mood	ما عندي مزاج
mish ' ala baali	I don't feel like it	مش على بالي
laTeef	nice	لطيف

43 - Household Vocabulary

Household Vocabulary:		مفردات عن البيت mufradaat ' an l bayt
bayt	House	بيت
shiqqa	Apartment	شقة
Taabiq	Floor	طابق
Hadiiqa	Garden	حديقة
Salon	Living Room	صالون
maktab	Office	مكتب
maTbakh	Kitchen	مطبخ
Himmaam	Bathroom	حمّام
ghurfit Ta'aam	Dining Room	غرفة طعام
oudhit sufra	Dining room	اوضة سفرة
ghurfit julus	Family Room	غرفة جلوس
balcon	Terrace	بلكون
ghurfit naoum	Bed Room	غرفة نوم
Tawlit sufra	Dining Table	طاولة سفرة
kirsi	Chair	كرسي
miftaaH	key	مفتاح
baab	Door	باب
shibbaak	Window	شباك
Sijjaadi	Carpet	سجادة
Birdaayi	Blinds/ curtain	برداية
takht	Bed	تخت
mkhaddi	Pillow	مخدّة

sharshaf	Sheet	شرشف
Hraam	Blanket	حرام
farshi	Mattress	فرشي
manshafi	Towel	منشفة
Saabouni	Soap	صابونة
firshaayet asnaan	Toothbrush	فرشاية أسنان
mushT	Comb	مشط
shafra	Razor	شفرة
SaHn	Dish	صحن
shawki	Fork	شوكة
mal 'aqa	Spoon	ملعقة
sikkiin	Knife	سكّين
Qass	to Cut	قصّ
mishwi	Grilled	مشوي
miqli	Fried	مقلي
miHshi	Stuffed	محشي
maslooq	Boiled	مسلوق
maTboukh	Cooked	مطبوخ
furn	Oven	فرن
finjaan	cup	فنجان
Tanjara	Pot	طنجرة
miqli	Pan	مقلي
jaaT	Bowl	جاط
oudha	room	أوضة
oudhit sufra	dining room	اوضة سفرة
HayT	wall	حيط
majroor	sewer	مجرور
daraj	stairs	درج
birdaayee	curtain	بردايي

kirsit Himmaam	toilette	كرسة حمّام
douch	shower	دوش
Maghsali	sink	مغسلة
Hanafiyyi	tap	حنفية
birki	pool	بركة
sa'f/saqf	roof	سقف
saTH	ceiling	سطح
'atabi	threshold	عتبة
Ifl/qifl	lock	قفل
miftaaH	key	مفتاح
armeed	bricks	قرميد
majlaa	kitchen sink	مجلى
lHaaf	quilt	لحاف
madkhal	entrance	مدخل
manfadha	ashtray	منفضة
ghissali	washer	غسالة
nishaafi	dryer	نشافة
jillaayyi	dishwasher	جلاية
burraad	fridge	براد
tillaaji	freezer	تلاجة
boutagaaz	gas stove	بوتاغاز
mikinsi	broom	مكنسة
mamsaHa	mop	ممسحة
rakwi	coffee pot	ركوة
SaHn	dish	صحن
Naar	fire	نار
Saniyyi	tray	صنيّة
maTHani	grinder	مطحنة

shawbak	rolling pin	شوبك
im '/ qim '	funnel	قمع
kibbaayi	glass	كبّاية
mamlaHa	salt shaker	مملحة
malqaT	tong	ملقط
minkhul	sieve	منخل
manfadha	ashtray	منفضة
idri/ qidri	pot	قدري

44 - Fruit and Such

Fruit and such	fwaaki	فواكة
fwaaki	Fruit	فواكه
tiffaaH	Apples	تفاح
'inab	Grapes	عنب
teen	Figs	تين
mawz	Bananas	موز
rimmaan	Pomegranate	رمان
khawkh	Plums	خوخ
dirraaq	peaches	دراق
mushmush	Apricots	مشمش
shimmaam	Canaloupe	شمّام
baTTikh	watermelon	بطيخ
fraaz	Strawberries	فراز
laymoon	Oranges	ليمون
injaas	Pears	نجاص
tamr	Dates	تمر
mushmush	Apricots	مشمش
tout	mulberry	توت
kharroub	carob	خروب
khawkh	plums	خوخ
mawz	bananas	موز

45 - Nuts

Nuts	mkassaraat	مكسرات
lawz	Almond	لوز
jawz	Walnut	جوز
fistouq	Peanut	فستق
bizr	Seeds	بزر
fistouq Halabi	Pistachio	فستق حلبي
bindouq	hazelnut	بندق
jawz	walnut	جوز
kastanaa	chestnut	كستناء
lawz	almond	لوز

46 - Vegetables

Khudhra	vegetables	خضره
baSal	onions	بصل
toom	garlic	توم
ba'dounis	parsley	بقدونس
Haamodh	lemon/lime	حامض
sfarjal	quince	سفرجل
baami	okra	بامي
lift	turnip	لفت
flayfli	pepper	فليفله
za 'tar	thyme	زعتر

sbaanikh	spinach	سبانخ
shmandar	beet	شمندر
ar '	pumpkin	قرع
kuzbara	coriander	كزبره
baTaTa	potato	بطاطا
banadoura	tomatoes	بندوره
khass	lettuce	خسّ
khiyaar	cucumber	خيار
baqdounis	parsley	بقدونس
na 'na '	mint	نعنع
fijel	radish	فجل
malfoof	cabbage	ملفوف
batinjaan	eggplant	باتنجان
kousa	squash	كوسى
arnabiiT	cauliflower	قرنبيط
silq	Swiss chard	سلق
'adas	lentils	عدس
burgul	crushed wheat	برغل
Hummous	Garbanzo beans	حمّص
fasolia	lima beans	فاصوليا
bazella	peas	بازيلا
fool	fava beans	فول
TaHiin	flour	طحين
khamiiri	yeast	خميرة
amH	wheat	قمح
turmus	lupine	ترمس
sh 'iir	barley	شعير
shoufaan	oats	شوفان

47- Coffee

Ahwi / Qahwi	coffee	قهوة
bann	coffee beans	بنّ
yiTHan	to grind	يطحن
Hilwi	sweet	حلوي
murra	bitter	مرّه
wasaT	medium	وسط
bidoun sukkar	without sugar	بدون سكر
ma ' sukkar	with sugar	مع سكر
shway sukkar	little sugar	شوي سكر
ma' haal	with cardamom	مع هال
bidoun haal	without cardamom	بدون هال
mighliyyi mniiH	boiled well	مغليي منيح
kiif bitHib al ahwi? How do you like the coffee? كيف بتحب القهوه		
Itfadhal. say it when you offer the coffee: please accept this offering تفضّل		
ahla wsahla	you are welcome	أهلا وسهلا
ahwi taaza	fresh coffee	قهوة تازة
shaay	tea	شاي
Jins	kind/type	― جنس
naw '	kind/type	― نوع
bala	without	بلا
bala sukkar	without sugar	بلا سكر

48 - Clothing

Clothing	tiyaab	تياب
amiis	shirt	قميص
banTaloon	pants	بنطلون
fustaan	woman's dress	فستان
tannoura	Skirt	تنوره
blooza	Blouse	بلوزه
Subbaat	Man's shoes	صبّات
jazma	Boots	جزمه
krafaat	Necktie	كرافات
qshaaT	Belt	قشاط
jakate	Jacket	جاكيت
badli	Suit	بدله
birnayTa	Hat	برنيطة
kfoof	Gloves	كفوف
'waynaat	Eye Glasses	عوينات
kalsaat	Socks	كلسات
skarbini	Woman's shoes	سكربينة
kanzi	Sweater	كنزة
jizdaan	Purse	جزدان
shaal	Scarf	شال
mihfaza	Wallet	محفظة
shirwaal	traditional baggy pants	شروال
Tarboosh	traditional man's hat	طربوش
kabbout	overcoat	كبّوت
kalsaat	socks	كلسات
maHrami	handkerchief	محرمة
mitr	measuring tape	متر
uTn/ quTn	cotton	قطن

49 - The Body

aljism	the body:	الجسم
raas	head	راس
sha 'r	hair	شعر
jbiin	forehead	جبين
Haajib/Hawaajib	eyebrow	حاجب
anf = minkhaar	nose	انف ـ منخار
'ayn/ 'aynayn/	eye	عين
tim	mouth	تمّ
shfaaf	lips	شفاف
lisaan	tongue	لسان
sin/asnaan	tooth	سن
wijj	face	وجّ ـ وجه
khad/ khudoud	cheek	خدّ
daqn	chin	دقن
Raqbi/ra'bi	neck	رقبي
kitf/ aktaaf	shoulder	كتف
eed/eedayn	hand	إيد
Kou '	elbow	كوع
iSba '/ Saabi '	finger	اصبع
dufr/ adaafer	nail	ضفر
baTn	belly	بطن
mi 'di	stomach	معدي
dhahr	back	ضهر
fakhdh	thigh	فخذ
ijr/ ijrayn	leg	اجر
rikbi	knee	ركبي
kaaHil	ankle	كاحل
qalb – alb	heart	قلب

dayni	ear	ديني
jild	skin	جلد
khaSr	waist	خصر
damm	blood	دم
dmaagh	brain	دماغ
riyya	lung	ريّا
snaan	teeth	سنان
sinn	tooth	سنّ
shwaarib	moustache	شوارب
'adhm	bone	عضم
liHyyi	beard	لحيي
bawl	urine	بول
taHleel	analyses	تحليل
Surit ashi 'a	x ray	صورة اشعا
kilwee	kidney	كلوة
Hasaasiyyi	allergy	حساسية
nabdh	pulse	نبض
rouchetta	prescription	روشاتا
waSaf	to prescribe	وصف
jourH	wound	جرح
Nazeef	bleeding	نزيف
Dawkhaa	dizziness	دوخة
salaTaan	cancer	سلطان
Istifraagh	vomiting	استفراغ
Sukkary	diabetes	سكّري
maT 'oum	vaccine	مطعوم

50 - What Do You Eat At the Restaurant?

shu btaakul bil maT 'am	what do you eat at the restaurant	شو بتاكل بالمطعم؟
maazaat	appetizers	مازات
tabbouli	traditional Lebanese salad	تبولي
kibbi nayyi	raw kibbi	كبّي نيي
kibbi mishwiyii	grilled kibbi	كبّي مشويي
laHm mishwi	grilled meat	لحم مشوي
farrouj mishwi	grilled young chicken	فروج مشوي
djaaj mishwi	grilled chicken	دجاج مشوي
slaaTa	salad	سلاطة
Hummous	paste chick peas	حمّص
tirweeqa/tirwee'a	breakfast	ترويقة
ghadaa	lunch	غدا
'ashaa	dinner	عشا
'aSrouniyyi	afternoon snack	عصرونية
shourba	soup	شوربا
sukkar	sugar	سكّر
milH	salt	ملح
bhaar	pepper	بهار
mraTTabaat	beverages	مرطبات
khudhra	vegetables	خضرا
fwaaki	fruit	فواكة
Fattouche	mixed salad with bread	فتوش
faatoura	bill	فاتورة
mashroobaat	drinks	مشروبات
kuHul	alcohol	كحول

Tabbaakh	cook	طبّاخ
baba ghannouj	eggplant with tahini sauce	بابا غنوج
samak mishwi	grilled fish	سمك مشوي
samak miqli	fried fish	سمك مقلي
falaafil	vegetatian meatball	فلافل
shawerma khaarof	skewered lamb	شاورما خروف
shawerma djaaj	skewered chicken	شاورما دجاج
laHm	meat	لحم
khaarouf	lamb	خروف
baqar/ba'ar	beef	بقر
khanzeer	pork	خنزير
kabiis	pickles	كبيس
khibz	bread	خبز
furn	bakery	فرن
khibz furn	bakery bread	خبّز فرن
khibz Saaj	mountain thin bread	خبز صاج
manqushi	flat bread	منقوشي
manqushit za 'tar	flat bread with thyme & olive oil	منقوشة زعتر
baydh	eggs	بيض
miqli	fried	مقلي
maslouq	boiled	مسلوق
manqushit laHm bi 'ajiin	flat bread with meat	منقوشة لحم بعجين
zayt	oil	زيت

khall	vinegar	خلّ
zaytoun	olives	زيتون
fwaaki	fruit	فواكه
Hilwaayaat	sweets	حلويات
knaafi	famous Lebanese sweet for breakfast	كنافة t
baqlaawa	famous Lebanese sweet	بقلاوة
qashTa	cream	قشطة
riz bHaliib	rice in milk	رز بحليب
dibs	carob syrop	دبس
mrabba	jam/jelly	مربّى
'asal	honey	عسل
Halaawi	tahini & sugar extract	حلاوة
bouza	ice cream	بوظة
ma 'moul	paste with nuts	معمول
TaHini	sesame sauce	طحينة
shokolaata	chocolate	شوكولاته
mayy ma 'daniyyi	mineral water	مي معدنية
kaasak	cheers	كاسك
gaato	cake	كَاتو
labni	strained yougart	لبنة
Haliib	milk	حليب
laban	yogurt	لبن
jibnee	cheese	جبنة
'araq- arak, traditional Lebanese liquor distilled from grape juice with anisette 100% proof		عرق
beera	beer	بيرا
wiski	whisky	وسكي
nbeed	wine	نبيد
'aSeer	juice	عصير

84

mayy	water	مي
kakaaw	cacao	كاكاو
kafta	ground lamb meat with parsley, tomatoe, spices	كفتة
Sheesh Taawook	skewered marinated chicken	شيش طاووق
laHm nay	raw meat	لحم ني

51- What Do You Do?

shu bta 'mil /// shu btishtighil? you do?	what do	شوب تعمل \ شوب تشتغل
waziifi	job	وظيفة
mihni	profession	مهنة
muwazzaf	employee	موظف
istaaz	teacher	استاز
muHaami	lawyer	محامي
taajir	merchant	تاجر
boliis	police	بوليس
doctor	doctor	دكتور
Tayyarji	pilot	طيرجي
liHHaam	butcher	لحّام
nijjaar	carpenter	نجّار
Hiddaad	blacksmith	حداد
jawharji	jeweler	جوهرجي
sankari	plumber	سنكري
fannaan	artist	فنان
rassaam	painter	رسّام
shaa 'ir	poet	شاعر
kaatib	writer	كاتب
khibbaaz	baker	خبّاز
farraan	baker	فران
taajir	merchant	تاجر
Sarraaf	money exchanger	صراف
mi 'marji	builder	معمرجي
muwazzaf bank	bank employee	موظف بنك
muwazzaf shirki	company employee	موظف شركي

muwazzaf Hukumi	government employee	موظف حكومي
SaaHib shirki	company owner	صاحب شركي
SaaHib maHal	store owner	صاحب محل
khidharji	grocer	خضرجي
mitqaa 'id	retired	متقاعد
Mitmawwil	independently wealthy	متموّل
Tabbaakh	cook	طباخ
kindarji	shoe repair	كندرجي
shiHHaad	beggar	شحاد
mhandis	engineer	مهندس
Ahwaji	coffee shop owner	قهوجي
niswanji	womanizer	نسونجي
bostaji	mailman	بوسطجي
iTfa'ji	fireman	اطفأجي
billaaT	tile man	بلاط
kihrabji	electrician	كهربجي
mudeer	director	مدير
Shagheel	laborer	شغيل
faa 'il	laborer	فاعل
dihhaan	painter	دهان
Saydali	pharmacist	صيدلي
jirraaH	surgeon	جراح
Tabbaakh	cook	طبّاخ
Tabeeb asnaan	dentist	طبيب اسنان
Tabeeb bayTary	veterinary	طبيب بيطري
Hakeem	doctor/ MD	حكيم
SaHafee	journalist	صحافي
ra'aaSa/ raqqaaSa	dancer (f)	رقاصة
mSawwir	photographer	مصور
muHaami	lawyer	محامي

qaadhi/aadhi	judge	قاضي
mHaasib	accountant	محاسب
m 'allim	teacher	معلّم
muTrib	singer	مطرب
mumathil	actor	ممثل

52 - Animals

Hayawaanaat	animals	حيوانات
Hayawaan	animal	حيوان
kalb	dog	كلب
bsayni	cat	بسينة
faara	mouse	فارة
jardoun	rat	جردون
HSaan	horse	حصان
Hmaar	donkey	حمار
baghl	mule	بغل
asad	lion	اسد
nimr	tiger	نمر
ba'ara	cow	بقرة
khaarouf	lamb	خروف
timsaaH	crocodile	تمساح
tawr	bull	تور
arnab	rabbit	ارنب
ghazaal	deer	غزال
Hayyee	snake	حيّة
' aqrab	scorpion	عقرب
boum	owl	بوم
ta 'lab	fox	تعلب
Jamal	camel	جمل
khanzeer	pig	خنزير
dibb	bear	دب
deeb	wolf	ديب

samaki	fish	سمكة
'anzi	goat	عنزة
Feal	elephant	فيل
ird/qird	monkey	قرد
djaaji	chicken	دجاجة
deek	rooster	ديك
'asfoor	bird	عصفور
fraashi	butterfly	فراشة
deek Habash	turkey	ديك حبش
nisr	eagle	نسر
Hout	whale	حوت
Hanklees	eel	حنكليس
karkadan	lobster	كركدن
dibbaani	fly	دبّانة
Hirbaayee	chameleon	حربايي
doudi	worm	دودة
dabbour	wasp	دبّور
naHli	bee	نحلة
SarSour	roach	صرصور
fraashi	butterfly	فراشة
namli	ant	نملة

53- Jewelry

mujawharaat	jewelry	مجوهرات
Siigha	jewelry	صيغة
dahab	gold	دهب
ilmaaz	diamond	الماز
fayrouz	turquoise	فيروز
fidhaa	silver	فضة
khaatim	ring	خاتم
iswaara	bracelet	اسوارة
saa 'a	watch	ساعة
Halaq	earings	حلق
'aqd	necklace	عقد
Jawharji	jeweler	جوهرجي
souq alsiyyaghiin	jewelry market	سوق الصياغين
hdiyye	gift	هدية
ghaali	expensive	غالي
rkheeS	cheap	رخيص
Hilou	beautiful	حلو
mish Hilou	not beautiful	مش حلو
kbeer	big	كبير
Sgheer	small	صغير
waasi '	wide	واسع
dayyi'	tight	ضيّق
mnaasib	suitable	مناسب
'al add	just right	عال قد
ti'leed	imitation	تقليد
Saafee	pure	صافي
maHbas	engagement ring	محبس

54 - In the News

in the news	bil akhbaar	بالأخبار
akhbaar	news	أخبار
radio	radio	راديو
televizion	television	تلفزيون
telephone	telephone	تلفون
telephone jawwaal	cell phone	تلفون جوا
khilyawi	cell phone	خليوي
naqqaal	cell phone	نقال
khaTT	line	خط
nimra	number	نمرة
raqm	number	رقم
shou nimrit taliphonak? What is your phone number شو نمرة تلفونك؟		
muzii '	announcer	مزيع
nashrit akhbaar	newscast	نشرة اخبار
qanaat	channel	قناة
shaashi	screen	شاشة
moujaz	brief	موجز
moujaz akhbaar	news brief	موجز اخبار
tafaaSeel	details	تفاصيل
khabar 'aajil	breaking news	خبر عاجل
saHafa	press	صحافة
saHaafi	journalist	صحافي
jareedi	newspaper	جريدة
saHeefee	newspaper	صحيفة
'inwaan	headline	عنوان
maqaal	article	مقال

mkhaabara	phone call	مخابرة
dawliyee	international	دوليّة
waTan	homeland	وطن
isti'laal	independence	استقلال
intikhaab	election	انتخاب
barlamaan	parliament	برلمان
taSweet	voting	تصويت
jamhouriyyi	republic	جمهورية
mamlaki	kingdom	مملكة
imaara	emirate	امارة
Hizb	party	حزب
Siyaasi	politics	سياسة
Hizb siyaasi	political party	حزب سياس
safaara	embassy	سفارة
safeer	ambassador	سفير
Jaysh	army	جيش
'aaSmi	capital	عاصمة
qunSul	consul	قنصل
qunSuliyyi	consulate	قنصلية
malak	king	ملك
amiir	prince	امير
ra'iis	president	رئيس
mu'tamar	conference	مؤتمر
mu'tamar SuHufi	press conference	مؤتمر صحفي
waziir	minister	وزير
naayeb	parliament member	نايب
wizaara	ministry/government	وزارة
ra'iis al wizaara	prime minister	رئيس الوزارة
wizaarit al khaarijiyee	ministry of foreign affairs/ state department	وزارة الخارجية

wizaarit al daakhiliyee	ministry of the interior	وزارة الداخلية
wizaarit al difaa '	ministry of defense	وزارة الدفاع
dharaaib	taxes	ضرائب
mujrim	criminal	مجرم
liSS	thief	لصّ
sir'a/sirqa	theft	سرقة
Haraami	thief	حرامي
Habs	jail	حبس
man ' altajawwul	curfew	منع التجول
teknologia	technology	تكنولوجي
wasaa'l al i 'laam	media	وسائل الاعلام
izaa 'a	radio station	ازاعة
Sawt	voice/sound	صوت
SaHafi	press/ media	صحافة
Jareedi	newspaper	جريدة
majalli	magazine	مجلة
malaff	file	ملف
Mawqi '	website	موقع
Qanaat	channel	قناة
i 'laan	advertisement	اعلام
barnaamaj	program	برنامج
muraasil	correspondent	مراسل
muzii '	announcer	مزيع
mu'tamar SuHufi	press conference	مؤتمر صحفي
taqreer/ta'reer	report	تقرير
bath Haay/mubaashar	live broadcast	بث حي – مباشر
musalsal	program/ soap opera	مسلسل
Hala'a	episode	حلقة
waadhiH	clear	واضح

kilmit sir	password	كلمة سر
mushaahid	viewer	مشاهد
mustami '	listener	مستمع
ajnabee	foreigner	اجنبي
ajaanib	foreigners	أجانب
ba 'du	he is still (doing something)	بعدو
akkad	to confirm	أكّد
nafaa	to deny	نفى
nakar	to deny	نكر
SarraH	to declare	صرّح
ra'i	opinion	رأي
ra'yii	my opinion	رأيي
sharaH	to explain	شرح
jaawab	to respond	جاوب
jawaab	respons	جواب
istajwab	to interrogate	استجوب
istafham	to inquire	استفهم
lammaH	to hint	لمّح
samaH	to allow	سمح
rafadh	to refuse	رفض
waafaq	to agree	وافق
shaarak	to participate	شارك
iktashaf	to discover	اكتشف
sabbab	to cause	سبّب
natiiji	result	نتيجة
istafaad	to benefit	استفاد
'alanan	publicly	علناً
bilsir	in secret	بالسر
bifadhl	thanks to	بفضل
dharouri	necessary	ضروري

mish dharouri	not necessary	مش ضروري
laazim	must – necessary	لازم
mustaHiil	impossible	مستحيل
mumkin	possible	ممكن
qaraar/araar	decision	قرار
khuTTa	plan	خطّة
ma 'loumaat	information	معلومات
istikhbaaraat	intelligence	استخبارات
munaasabi	occasion	مناسبة
mawqif	position	موقف
ToumouH	ambition	طموح
mitfaa'il	optimistic	متفائل
mitshaa'im	pessimistic	متشائم
' aadi	ordinary	عادي
kaamil	complete	كامل
mashhour	famous	مشهور
khaaS	private	خاص
' aam	public	عام
bi asra ' waqt	as soon as possible	باسرع وقت
'aadatan	usually	عادة
daayman	always	دايماً
aHyaanan	sometimes	أحياناً
khilaal	during	خلال
al Saleeb al aHmar	Red Cross	الصليب الأحمر
al hilaal al aHmar	Red Crescent	الهلال الأحمر
irhaab	terrorism	إرهاب
thawra	revolution	ثورة
Mufaawadhaat	negotiations	مفاوضات
naSiiHa	advice	نصيحة
tawattur	tension	توتّر

ighteeyaal	assassination	إغتيال
Harb	war	حرب
silm/salaam	peace	سلام
Haajiz	road block	حاجز
shaheed	martyr	شهيد
irhaabi	terrorist	ارهابي
irhaab	terror	ارهاب
muHaawalit ightiyaal	assassination attempt	محاولة اغتيال
Mujrim	criminal	مجرم

55 - At the Post Office

At the post office	bi maktab al bareed	مكتب البريد
Taabi'	stamp	طابع
Tawaabi '	stamps	طوابع
maktoub	letter	مكتوب
risaali	letter	رسالة
mista 'jil	urgent	مستعجل
Sandouq bareed	P.O. Box	صندوق بريد
zarf	envelope	ظرف
'inwaan	address	عنوان
Idraas	address	ادراس
Tard	parcel	طرد
barqiyyee	telegram	برقية
maktoub msawkar	registered mail	مكتوب مسوكر
madhmoon	certified	مضمون
waSl	receipt	وصل
mghallaf	envelope	مغلف
bostagee	mail man	بوسطجي
ma 'aash	salary	معاش
maktab albareed	post office	مكتب البريد
baladiyye	municipality	بلدية
ra'ees albaladiyye	mayer	رئيس البلدية
al mukhtaar	town official	المختار

'udhu	member	عضو
rukhSa	permit	رخصة
rukhSit 'amaar/ binaa	building permit	رخصة عمار – بنا
rukhSit tarmeem	renovation permit	رخصة ترميم
istiqaali	resignation	استقالة
ta 'yeen	appointment	تعيين
intikhaab	election	انتخاب

56 - At the Tailor

at the tailor	'ind al khiyyaaT	عند الخيّاط
eeyaas	measurement	أياس
khiyyaaT	tailor	خياط
badlee	suit	بدلة
fistaan	dress	فستان
zirr	button	زرّ
tannoura	skirt	تنّورة
kimm	sleeve	كمّ
abbee	color	أبّة
maazoora	measuring tape	مازورة
qmaash/'maash	material	قماش
joukh	wool	جوخ
Hareer	silk	حرير
moodha	fashion	موضة
Jaybee	pocket	جيبي
kanzi	sweater	كنزة
Souf	wool	صوف
oTn/qoTn	cotton	قطن

57- At the Barber/Hairdresser

At the Barber	'ind al Hillaaq	عند الحلاق
Na 'iman	may you enjoy it	نعيماً
Yin 'am 'alayk	response to above quote	ينعم عليك
uss	to cut	قصّ
sha 'r	hair	شعر
saawi	fix/ style	ساوي
uSbough	dye/ color	أصبغ
swaalif	side burns	سوالف
iHlo'/iHloq	shave	احلق
da'n/daqn	chin	دقن
wijj	face	وجّ – وجه
liHyyi	beard	لحية
shwaarib	moustache	شوارب
Taweel	long	طويل
aSeer	short	قصير
Saaboun	soap	صابون
Shafra	razor	شفرة
mushT	comb	مشط
moose	shaving razor	موسى
ghassil	wash	غسّل
mashiTT	to comb	مشّط
shampoo	shampoo	شامبو
ceshwaar	hair dryer	سشوار
spray	hairspray	سبراي
ma 'joun Hlaaqa	shaving cream	معجون حلاقة

58 - At the Supermarket

bil supermarket	at the supermarket	بالسوبر ماركت
laazimni	I am in need of	لازمني
ishtiri	to buy	اشتري
marHaba	hello	مرحبا
min fadhlak	please	من فضلك
i 'mul ma 'rouf	do me a favor	اعمول معروف
iza bitreed	if you please	إزا بتريد
i 'Tini	give me	اعطيني
baddi	I want	بدّي
kilou	kilo	كيلو
niss kilou	half a kilo	نصّ كيلو
tlati kilou	three kilos	تلاتي كيلو
ouqiyyi	pound	اوقية
rib ' ouqiyyi	quarter pound	ربع اوقية
niss ouqiyyi	half pound	نصّ اوقية
ouqitayn	two pounds	اوقيتين
rabTa	stack/ bundle	ربطة
' ilbi	box	علبة
kees	bag	كيس
dazzini	dozen	دزينة
iddaysh al kilou?	How much	اديش الكيلو
bikam al kilou?	How much	بكم الكيلو
meezaan	scale	ميزان
burraad	fridge	براد
baarid	cold	بارد
annini	bottle	قنينة
dikkaan	small shop	دكان

'arabiyyi	cart	عربية
Sandooq	cashier	صندوق
chaak	check	تشاك
biTaqit visa	Visa card	بطاقة فيزا
cash	cash	كاش
naqdee/na'dee	cash	نقدي
dikhaan	tobacco/cigarettes	دخّان
'ilbit dikhaan	pack of cigarettes	علبة دخان
kroze dikhaan	box of cigarettes	كروز دخان
ghaali	expensive	غالي
Rkhees	cheap	رخيص
ridd	return	ردّ
ibdul	exchange	ابدل

59 - At the Bookstore

bil maktabi مكتبة	at the bookstore – library	
ktaab	book	كتاب
daftar	notebook	دفتر
kutub	books	كتب
dafaater	notebooks	دفاتر
masTara	ruler	مسطرة
alam Hibr	ink pen	قلم حبر
alam rSaaS	pencil	قلم رصاص
Hibr	ink	حبر
aqlaam	pens	اقلام
wara'a	paper	ورقة
awraaq	papers	اوراق
miHHaayi	eraser	محاية
maHbara	ink pot	محبرة
Tawli	table/desk	طاولة
lawH	blackboard	لوح
sabboura	blackboard	سبّورة
fardh	homework	فرض
waajib bayti	homework	واجب بيتي
raff	shelf	رفّ
sillum	ladder	سلّم
aakhud	take	آخد
ista 'iir	borrow	استعير

rajji '	return	رجّع
iqra/ i'ra	read	اقرا
isma '	listen	اسمع
shoof	see	شوف
Tabshour	chalk	طبشور
Qaamous	dictionary	قاموس
QiSSa/iSSa	story	قصّة
qaSidee/ aSidee	poem	قصيدة
khareeTa	map	خريطة

60 - At the Restaurant

bil maT 'am	at the restaurant	بالمطعم
ahla wsahla	welcome	أهلا وسهلا
Itfadhal	please come in/ please take this	تفضل
Tawli	table	طاولة
Hadd	near	حدّ
Janb	near	جنب
shibbaak	window	شبّاك
garson	waiter	غارسون
khaadim	server	خادم
SaHn yawmi	daily special	صحن يومي
laa'iHat alTa 'aam	menu	لائحة الطعام
shou bitHib	what do you want	شو بتحب
akl	food	اكل
shou bitHib taakul?	What do you like to eat	شو بتحب تاكل
shou 'ala baalak?	What are you in the mood for	شو على بالك
tikram you are welcome(response to I want…)		تكرم
tikram 'aynak	same as above	تكرم عينك
amrak	at your service	أمرك
shu b tu'mur	what do you want to order	شو بتأمر
ya sidi	sir	يا سيدي
arkili	water pipe	اركيلي
tanbak	tobacco	تنبك
jamra	charcoal	جمرة
shu al Hisaab?	What is the balance	شو الحساب
faatoora	bill	فاتورة
bakhsheesh	tip	بخشيش
barTeel	bribery	برطيل

61- At the Coffee Shop

bil ahwi	at the coffee shop	ب الأهوي - القهوة - المقهى
finjaan	cup	فنجان
ahwi	coffee	اهوي - قهوة
shaay	tea	شاي
sigaara	cigarette	سيكارة
ghalyoon	pipe	غليون
arkili	water pipe	اركيلي
dikhaan	tobacco	دخان
Taawlit zahr	backgammon	طاولة زهر
wara'	cards	ورق
yil 'ab	to play	يلعب
shaTaranj	chess	شطرنج
tasliyi	entertainment	تسلية

62- At the Bank

bil bank	at the bank	بالبنك
chaak	check	تشاك
daftar chaakaat	check book	دفتر تشاكات
Hisaab	account	حساب
Hisaab jaari	checking account	حساب جاري
Hisaab tawfeer	savings account	حساب توفير
iftaH	to open	افتح
sakkir	to close	سكّر
raSiid	balance	رصيد
idfa '	to pay	ادفع
uSruf	to cash/ spend	اصرف
HuTT	put/ deposit	حطّ
isHab	to withdraw	اسحب
Hawwil	to transfer	حوّل
baddi iftaH Hisaab jdiid I want to open a new account بدي افتح حساب جديد		
zboon	customer	زبون
mu 'aamali	transaction	معاملة
fir '	branch	فرع
maSaari	money	مصاري
'imli Sa 'bi	hard currency	عملة صعبة
al bourSa	the stock market	البورصة
HiSaS	shares	حصص
ashum	shares	اسهم
Souq	market	سوق
Taali '	up	طالع
naazil	down	نازل

khisaara	loss	خسارة
ribH	gain	ربح
na'di	cash	نقدي
dayn	debt	دَين
raas almaal	capital	راس المال
iflaas	bankruptcy	إفلاس
raqm al Hisaab	account number	رقم الحساب
chaak bidoun raSeed	bounced check	تشاك بدون رصيد
bidoun	without	بدون
wakaali	power of attorney	وكالة
kafaali	guarantee/sponsorship	كفالة
Hwaali	money order	حوالة
Imdhaa	signature	إمضاء
Tawqee '	signature	توقيع
Faaydee	interest	فايدة

63 - At the Airport

Bil maTaar	at the airport	بالمطار
maTaar	airport	مطار
Tiyyara	airplane	طيّارة
Tiyarji	pilot	طيرجي
ajnabi	foreigner	أجنبي
madraj	runway	مدرج
Hajz	reservation	حجز
isti 'laamaat	information	إستعلامات
baHr	sea	بحر
ardh	land	ارض
barr	land	برّ
Jaw	air	جو
mudhiifi	stewardess	مضيفة
paspor	passport	بسبور
visa	visa	فيزا
ta'shiirit dukhul	visa	تأشيرة دخول
middit	duration of time	مدّة
min wayn?	From where	مِن وين؟
Iddaysh baddak tibqa hawn? How long do you want to stay here?		اديش بدك تبقى هون؟
miin 'indak hawn?	Whom do you have here?	مين عندك هون؟
shu sabab ziyartak?	Reason for your visit?	شو سبب زيارتك ؟
siyaaHa	tourism	سياحة
shighl	business	شغل
mamnoo '	forbidden	ممنوع
SarriH	declare	صرّح
tabyyidh amwaal	money laundering	تبييض اموال

wusoul	arrival	وصول
khurooj	exit/ departure	خروج
ta'khiir	delay	تأخير
izdiHaam	crowdedness	ازدحام
mughadara	departure	مغادرة
siyaHa	tourism	سياحة
saayeH	tourist	سايح
ziyaara	visit	زيارة
shighl	business	شغل
shanTa	suitcase	شنطة
shunaT	suitcases	شنط
dhaa 'it	was lost	ضاعت
wiSlit	arrived	وصلت
ma wiSlit	did not arrive	ما وصلت
miin ma ' ak?	Who is with you?	مين معك
waHdi	alone	وحدي
jaayii min	I am coming from	جايي مِن
raayeH ' a	I am going to	رايح ع
' inwaan	address	عنوان
idraas	address	ادراس
Talab	form	طلب
' abbi	fill out	عبّي
Imli	fill out	املي
Jamaarik	Customs	جمارك
al amn al 'aam	general security	الأمن العام
Fattish	to search	فتش
iftaH alshanTa	open the suitcase	افتح الشنطة
Hammaal	carrier/ porter	حمّال
bakhsheesh	tip	بخشيش
taxi	taxi	تاكسي

110

siyyarit ijra	service/ shared cab	سيارة اجرا
bosta	bus	بوسطة
shantit eed	hand bag	شنطة إيد
Soura	picture	صورة
muwaaTin	citizen	مواطن
laaji'	refugee	لاجئ
kart akhdhar	green card	كرت أخضر
jinsiyyi	citizenship	جنسيّة
bil Saff	in line	بالصف
aanoun/qaanoun	law	قانون
dhud al qaanoun	against the law	ضد القانون
wathiiqa	document	وثيقة
mas'ouliyyi	responsibility	مسؤولية
biTaaqit iqaami	residency card	بطاقة اقامة
iqaami	residency	اقامة
kaatib ' adl	notary public	كاتب عدل
middi	period of time/ duration	مدّة
tajdeed	renewal	تجديد
mulgha	canceled	ملغى
tamdeed	extension	تمديد
qaanoun/ aanoun	law	قانون
shurTee	policeman	شرطي
daraki	policemen	دركي
safar	travel	سفر
siyaaHa	tourism	سياحة
raHli	trip	رحلة
safeeni	ship	سفينة
meena	harbor	مينا
shaTT	shore	شطّ
Hajj	pilgrim	حاج

maq 'ad	seat	مقعد
sikkit Hadeed	railroad	سكّة حديد
tounaal	tunnel	تونال

64 - Traffic Issues

traffic issues	adhaaya al sayr	قضايا السير
shurTi muroor	traffic police	شرطي مرور
isharit wuqouf	stop sign	إشارة وقوف
sir 'aa	speed	سرعة
misri '	going fast/ speeding	مسرع
'ala mahlak	slow dowm	على مهلك
mukhalafi	violation	مخالفة
zabT	ticket	زبط
rikhsit swaaqa	driver's license	رخصة سواقة
awraaq alsiyyaara	car papers	اوراق السيارة
ta'meen	insurance	تأمين
shirki	company	شركة
dhamaan	insurance	ضمان
tasjeel	registration	تسجيل
Taqreer/ta'reer	report	تقرير

65 - Medical Vocabulary

medical vocabulary	مفردات طبية	mufradaat Tubbiyi
mistashfaa	hospital	مستشفى
Hakeem	doctor	حكيم
mumarridha	nurse	ممرضة
farmachaani	pharmacist	فرمشاني
Saydaliyyi	pharmacy	صيدلية
Saydali	pharmacist	صيدلي
dhamaan SuHHi	health insurance	ضمان صحي
SuHHa	health	صحّة
maradh	sickness	مرض
mareedh	sick	مريض
waja '	pain	وجع
alam	pain	الم
waja ' raas	headache	وجع راس
Ibree	shot/ needle	ابرة
miizaan Haraara	thermometer	ميزان حرارة
uTn/quTn	cotton	قطن
speerto	alcohol	سبيرتو
Tabeeb	doctor	طبيب
Hakiim	doctor	حكيم
siyyarit is 'aaf	ambulance	سيارة اسعاف
'amaliyyi	operation	عملية
tashkhiiS	diagnoses	تشخيص
jiraaHa	surgery	جراحة
banj	anesthesia	بنج
damm	blood	دم
Haadis	accident	حادث
dawaa	medicine	دوا

Habbi	pill	حبّة
Huboub	pills	حبوب
ta'meen/ dhamaan	insurance	تأمين – ضمان
is 'aafaat awaliyyi	first aid	إسعافات اولية
tiHmiili	suppository	تحميلة
aHHa	cough	قحّة
msakkin	tranquilizer	مسكّن
rashH	cold	رشح
sa 'li	cough	سعلة
iss haal	diarrhea	إسهال
imsaak	constipation	إمساك
ma 'joun asnaan	tooth paste	معجون أسنان
firshaayet asnaan	tooth brush	فرشاية أسنان
naa 'im	soft	ناعم
khishin	hard	خشن
Saaboon	soap	صابون
Haraara	temperature	حرارة
maHroor	with fever	محرور
Tabeeb ikhtiSaaSi	specialist	طبيب اختصاصي
waram	swelling	ورم
dhaghT damm	blood pressure	ضغط دم
'aTas	to sneeze	عطس
Hibli	pregnant	حبلي
maraa Hibli	pregnant woman	مرا حبلي
idmaan	addiction	إدمان
mudmin	addict	مدمن

66 - Hobbies

hiwaayaat	hobbies	هوايات
sibaaHa	swimming	سباحة
rakdh	running	ركض
ghawS	diving	غوص
rasm	painting	رسم
mashi	walking	مشي
musiiqa	music	موسيقى
qiraa'a	reading	قراءة
riyadhaa	sports	رياضة
tazalluj	skiing	تزلّج
Sayd al samak	fishing	صيد السمك
mSaara 'a	wrestling	مصارعة
mlaakami	boxing	ملاكمة

67 - Important Places

Important places	Amaakin muhimmi	أماكن مهمة
makaan	place	مكان
amaakin	places	اماكن
muhim	important	مهم
ishaara	sign	إشارة
dikkaan	small shop	دكّان
madeeni	city	مدينة
qaryyee	village	قرية
dhay 'a	town	ضيعة
otele	hotel	اوتيل
funduq	hotel	فندق
Tarii'	road	طريق
'amaara	building	عمارة
binaayyee	building	بناية
maT 'am	restaurant	مطعم
mHaTTit benzene	gas station	محطة بنزين
naadi	club	نادي
Hadeeqa	garden	حديقة
Jnayni	garden	جنينة
masraH	theater	مسرح
jisr	bridge	جسر
qaSr/aSr	palace	قصر
al 'a/qal 'a	castle	قلعة
mazra 'a	farm	مزرعة
jabal	mountain	جبل
izdiHaam	congestion	إزدحام

'aj'a/ 'ajqa	congestion/crowd	عجقة
Hayy	neighborhood	حي
manTaqa	district	منطقة
dhaaHiyyi	suburb	ضاحية
markaz	center	مركز
zaawi	corner	زاوية
talli	hill	تلّة
waadi	valley	وادي
supermarket	supermarket	سوبر ماركت
malHami	butcher house	ملحمة
manshara	carpentry place	منشرة
Hillaaq	barber shop	حلاق
ma 'Sara	oil press	معصرة
baladiyyi	municipality	بلدية
mujamma ' sakani	housing complex	مجمع سكني
maktab	office	مكتب
maktab albareed	post office	مكتب البريد
souq alkhudhra	vegetable market	سوق الخضرة
zaaroub	alley	زاروب
furn	bakery	فرن
ishaara	sign	اشارة
ishaarit muroor	traffic sign	اشارة مرور
ishaarit wooqouf	stop sign	اشارة وقوف
matHaf	museum	متحف
shaari ' raiisi	main street	شارع رئيسي
mustaddira	circle	مستديرة
moll	mall	مول

68 - How Do I Go to...?

wayn maktab al bareed? keef brouH 'al souq? وين مكتب البريد؟ كيف بروح عالسوق؟		
how do I go to the market?		
min fadhlak	please	من فضلك
wayn…	where (is)	وين
rouH	go	روح
dighrii	straight	دغري
'al yameen	to the right	عاليمين
'al shmaal	to the left	عالشمال
Hadd	near	حدّ
Urb/qurb	near	قرب
Janb	next to	جنب
iddaam	in front of	اددام
wara	behind	ورا
khalf	behind	خلف
fawq	above	فوق
taHt	below/ under	تحت
mqaabeel/m'aabeel	across from	مقابيل
bitchouf	you see	بتشوف
btooSal	you arrive at	بتوصل
mafraq/mafra'	crossroad/ intersection	مفرق
is'al	ask	اسأل
binaayyi	building	بناية
buwaab	doorman	بواب

69 - Countries' Sources of Income

maSaadir dakhl al balad the country's sources of income		مصادر دخل البلد
siyaaHa	tourism	سياحة
tijaara	trade/ commerce	تجارة
ziraa 'a	agriculture	زراعة
Sinaa 'a	manufacturing/ industry	صناعة
isteeraad	import	استيراد
taSdeer	export	تصدير
iqtiSaad	economy	اقتصاد
dharaa'ib	taxes	ضرائب
bay '	selling	بَيع
shiraa	buying	شِرا
mawaarid Tabii 'iyii	natural resources	موارد طبيعية
ashghaal ' aami	public works	اشغال عامة

70 - Sad Occassions

munaasabaat Hazini	sad occasions	مناسبات حزينة
mawt	death	موت
maat	he died	مات
maatit	she died	ماتت
'aTaak 'umru	he died	عطاك عمرو
twaffa	he died	توفى
jinnaaz	memorial service	جنّاز
ma'tam	funeral	مأتم
dafn	funeral	دفن
taabout	casket	تابوت
madfan	cemetary	مدفن
khoury	priest	خوري
irbaan	holy bread	قربان
iHdhar	to attend	احضر
'azzi	pay condolences	عزّي
ta 'aazi	condolences	تعازي
faqeed/fa'eed	deceased	فقيد
alla yirHamou	may God have mercy	الله يرحمو
al 'awadh bisalaamtak	pray for your safety	العوض بسلامتك

71 - My Daily Schedule

barnaamji al yawmi	my daily schedule	برنامجي اليومي
bou 'a	I wake up	بوعا
biSHa	I wake up	بصحا
kil yawm	every day	كل يوم
alsaa 'a	at (time)	الساعة
bakkeer	early	بكّير
mit'akhir	late	متأخر
bitHammam	I shower	بتحمم
bghassil wijji	I wash my face	بغسل وجهي
biHlo'/ biHloq	I shave	بحلق
b mashiTT sha 'ri	I comb my hair	بمشط شعري
b farshi snaani	I brush my teeth	بفرشي سناني
b nashiff sha 'ri	I dry my hair	بنشف شعري
bilbos tyaabi	I wear my clothes	بلبس تيابي
bitrawwaq	I have breakfast	بتروق
bi'ra al jareedi	I read the paper	بقرا الجريدة
bisma ' al akhbaar	I listen to the news	بسمع الأخبار
birkab bil siyyaara	I ride in the car	بركّب بالسيارة
brouH 'al shighl	I go to work	بروح عالشغل
bouSal 'al maktab	I arrive to the office	بوصل عالمكتب
biHdhar ijtimaa'	I attend a meeting	بحضر اجتماع
biHki 'al telefone	I speak on the phone	بحكي عالتلفون
ba 'mil maw 'id	I make an appointment	بعمل موعد
brouH 'al ghada	I go to lunch	بروح عالمكتب
bijtimi ' ma ' al mudeer	I meet with the director	بجتمع مع المدير
birja ' 'ala maktab	I return to the office	برجّع عالمكتب
bitruk al maktab	I leave the office	بترك المكتب

bzoor SaaHbi	I visit my friend	بزور صاحبي
minrouH 'al maT 'am	we go to the restaurant	منروح عالمطعم
mnit 'a shaa	we eat dinner	منتعشى
mnishrab kass	we have a drink	منشرب كاس
minrouH 'al sinama	we go to the movies	منروح عالسينما
birja ' 'al bayt	I return home	برجع عالبيت
biHdhar telefisyon	I watch TV	بحضر تلفزيون
b naam	I sleep	بنام

72 - Test Yourself

Test yourself:	امتحن نفسك	imtiHin nafsak
My uncle is tall/	' ammi Taweel	عمّي طويل
I want to eat rice in milk/ baddi aakul ruz ma ' Haleeb		بدي آكل رز مع حليب
I want boiled eggs/	baddi baydh maslouq	بدي بيض مسلوق
Where do you live?/	wayn saakin?	وين ساكن ؟
Who did you see today?/	meen shift al yawm?	مين شفت اليوم؟
Where are you from?/	min wayn inta?	من وين انت؟
What did you eat this morning?/ shu akalt 'abukra?		شو اكلت عبكرة ؟
How do I go to the post office? /keef brouH 'a maktab al bareed?	كيف بروح عمكتب البريد	
Where is the car?/	wayn al siyyara?	وين السيارة؟
My room is big/	ghurfti kbeeri/oudhti kbiri	اوضتي كبيرة
The library is far/	al maktabi b 'iidee	المكتبة بعيدة
She has a temperature/	'inda Haraara	عندا حرارة
My house is near the restaurant/ bayti Hadd al maT 'am		بيتي حد المطعم
His car is red/	siyyartu Hamra	سيارتو حمرا
This is a big city/	haydi mdini kbeeri	هيدي مدينة كبيرة
I am busy/	ana mashghul	انا مشغول
What is the capital of Lebanon?/shu 'aSmit libnaan?		شو عاصمة لبنان؟
We did not eat/	niHna ma akalnaa	نحن ما اكلنا
I have a green pen/	ma'i alam akhdhar	معي قلم اخضر
She likes to drink coffee/ hiyyi bitHib tishrab ahwi		هيي بتحب تشرب قهوي
How do you like your coffee?/ keef bitHib ahiwtak?		كيف بتحب قهوتك؟
The airplane is big/	alTiyyara kbiiri	الطيارة كبيرة
I want to buy a new suit/ baddi ishtiri badli jdeedi		بدي اشتري بدلة جديدة
Winter is long/	alshiti Taweel	الشتي طويل
Summer is hot/	alSayf Harr/ shawb	الصيف شوب

Spring is beautiful/	al rabii ' Hilou/jameel	الربيع حلو
You are welcome/	ahla w sahla feek	اهلا وسهلا فيك
Honored to meet you/	tsharrafna	تشرفنا
Good evening/	masa alkhayr	مسا الخير
What's going on?/	shou fee?	شو في
When do you want to go?	amteen baddak trouH?	امتين بدك تروح؟
See you tomorrow/	bshoufak bukra	بشوفك بكرا
Greetings my dear/	taHiyyati ya 'azizi	تحياتي يا عزيزي
Happy holiday/	'iid sa 'iid	عيد سعيد
I want to buy a gift/	baddi ishtiri hdiyyi	بدي اشتري هدية
Happy Palm Sunday/	sha 'nini sa 'iidi	شعنيني سعيدي
He went to church/	huwwi raaH 'al kneesi	هوي راح عالكنيسة
The mosque is far/	al jaami ' b 'iid	الجامع بعيد
The wedding was beautiful/	al 'urs kaan Hilou	العرس كان حلو
The bride is tall/	al 'arous Taweeli	العروس طويلة
The dog is outside/	al kalb barra	الكلب برا
What did he say?	Shou aal?	شو قال؟
Forgive me/	saamiHni	سامحني
He is an old man/	huwwi khityaar	هوي ختيار
He is getting younger/	huwwi mshabshib	هوي مشبشب
We played cards/	l 'ibna waraq	لعبنا ورق
Open the bottle of oil/	ftaaH aninit alzayt	فتاح قنينة الزيت
She drank juice/	hiyyi shirbit ' aSeer	هيي شربت عصير
He read the newspaper/	huwwi araa al jareedi	هوي قرا الجريدة
He forgot the appointment/	huwwi nisi al maw 'id	هوي نسي الموعد
I want to visit my relatives/	baddi zour araaybi	بدي زور قراييي
The weather was cold yesterday/	al Ta's kaan baarid mbaariH	الطقس كان بارد مبارح
The thief came at night/	alliSS ijaa billayl	اللص اجا بالليل
Tell me what do you want/	illi shou baddak	قلّي شو بدك
He has a headache/	'indu waja ' raas	عندو وجع راس

The shirt is small/	al amiiS Sghiree	القميص صغيرة
Beirut is the capital of Lebanon/	Beirut 'aaSmit libnaan	بيروت عاصمة لبنان
My nephew is an engineer/	ibn khayyi mhandis	ابن خيي مهندس
I want to rent an apartment/	baddi ista'jir shi'aa	بدي استأجر شقة
I want to buy a new house/	baddi ishtri bayt jdeed	بدي اشتري بيت جديد
I want a stamp for this letter/	baddi Taabi ' lil maktoub	بدي طابع للمكتوب
How do you go to the museum?/	keef bitrouH 'al matHaf?	كيف بتروح عالمتحف؟
Is the municipality open today?/	albaladiyyi faatHa al yawm?	البلدية فاتحا اليوم؟
My wife is a teacher/	marti istaazi/ m 'almi	مرتي معلمة
My husband went to the office/	jawzi raaH ' al maktab	جوزي راح عالمكتب
The airplane is late/	alTiyyara mit akhraa	الطيارة متأخرة
We ordered fried fish/	Talabna samak mi'li	طلبنا سمك مقلي
The economy is bad now/	al iqtiSaad sayyi' halla'	الاقتصاد سيء هلق
We want to travel to Europe/	badna nsaafir 'a oroppa	بدنا نسافر ع أوروبا
We attended a great party/	Hdhirna Hafli 'azimee	حضرنا حفلة عظيمة
I must rent a car/	laazim ista'jir siyyara	لازم استأجر سيارة
I love skiing and swimming/	bHibb altazallouj wil sibaaHa	بحب التزلج والسباحة
We ate breakfast at my uncle's house/	trawwaqna bi bayt 'ammi	تروقنا ببيت عمي
He died in an accident/	maat biHaadis	مات بحادث
He has a dog and a cat/	'indou kalb w bsayni	عندو كلب وبسينة
We had a house near the sea/	kaan 'inna bayt Hadd al baHr	كان عنا بيت حد البحر
They are our new neighbors/	hinni jiraanna lijdaad	هني جيرانا الجداد
The church is near the mosque/	al kneesi urb al jaami '	الكنيسة قرب الجامع
There was an earthquake in Brazil/	kaan fi zilzaal bil braaziil	كان في زلزال بالبرازيل
Syria is larger than Lebanon/	souriyya akbar min libnaan	سوريا اكبر من لبنان
I must go to the pharmacy to buy medicine/	laazim rouH 'al farmashiyyee Hatta ishtiri dawaa	لازم روح عالفرمشية حتى اشتري دوا
He is a poet and an artist/	huwwi shaa ' ir w fannaan	هوي شاعر وفنان

125

Do not pay attention. He is crazy/ maa tihtam, huwwi majnoun	ما تهتم. هوي مجنون
I am grateful/ mamnounak	ممنونك
The weather is rainy today/ al Ta's al yawn shiti	الطقس اليوم شتي
The storm is coming/ al 'aaSfi jaayee	العاصفة جايي
The river is deep/ al nahr ghamii'	النهر غميق
See you Tuesday/ bshoufak yawm al talaata	بشوفك يوم التلاتا
Two days ago/ min yawmayn	من يومين
Half an hour ago/ min niSS saa 'a	من نص ساعة
Lunch is at noon/ alghadaa 'al dhuhr	الغدا عالضهر
What time is it? Iddaysh al saa 'a?	اديش الساعة
Now or later?/ halla' aw ba 'daan?	هلق او بعدين؟
February is very cold/ shbaaT baarid kteer	شباط بارد كتير
My uncle is a lawyer/ 'ammi muHaami	عمي محامي
He is not married/ huwwi a 'zab/mish mitjawwiz	مش متجوز
She is a young woman/ hiyyi Sabiyyi	هيي صبيي
I want 25 books/ baddi khamsi w 'ishreen ktaab	بدي 25 كتاب
I saw a 1000 ships/ shift alf safeeni	شفت الف سفينة
His wife is rich/ martu ghaniyyi	مرتو غنيي
They are foreigners/ hinni ajaanib	هني اجانب
The road is here/ min hawn alTareeq	من هون الطريق
Where are you coming from/ min wayn jaayyii	من وين جايي
Where are you going to/ lawayn raayiH?	لوين رايح
Do you like to dance the Dabke? bitHib tur'ous dabki?	بتحب ترقص دبكي
Do you like Zajal? bitHib al zajal?	بتحب الزجل
shou ismak/ what is your name?	شو اسمك؟
keefak al yawm/ how are you today?	كيفك اليوم؟
tsharrafna/ honored to meet you	تشرفنا
iza allah raad/ if God willed so	اذا الله راد
min fadhlak wayn al maktab/ please. Where is the office?	من فضلك وين المكتب
ma ' meen kint/ who were you with?	مع مين كنت؟

shou fee bukra/	what is happening tomorrow?	شو في بكرا؟
mbaariH aw bukra?/	yesterday or tomorrow	مبارح او بكرا؟
salaam wa iHtiraam/	greetings and respect	سلام واحترام
wayn kint laylit raas al sini/where were you New Year's Eve?		وين كنت ليلة راس السنة؟
shou ijaak hadaaya?/	what gifts did you get?	شو اجاك هدايا؟
ramadhaan kareem ilak w lil 'ayli/ happy Ramadan to you and the family		رمضان كريم الك والعيلي
meen hayda, shaykh aw Khoury?/who is this, sheikh or priest?		مين هيدا، شيخ او خوري؟
al jaami ' b 'iid bas al kneesi ab 'ad/ the mosque is far but the church is farther		الجامع بعيد بس الكنيسة ابعد
riiHit al bakhour Hilwi/the smell of incense is sweet		ريحة البخور حلوي
shou ra'yak bil zawaaj al madani?/ your opinion on civil marriage		شو رأيك بالزواج المدني؟
keef kaan al 'urs?/	how was the wedding?	كيف كان العرس؟
kim walad 'indon?/	how many children do they have?	كم ولد عندن؟
fustaan al 'arus Hilou/	the bride's dress is beautiful	فستان العروس حلو
aalib al kaato kbeer/	the wedding cake is big	قالب الكاتو كبير
al ktaab fawq al Tawli/ the book is on the table		الكتاب فوق الطولي
al si 'r ghaali shwayy/ the price is a bit expensive		السعر غالي شوي
mish ma 'qoul ishtri hal siyyara/ it is impossible to buy this car		مش معقول اشتري هالسيارة
shou awlak minrouH 'al sinama/what do you think, shall we go to the cinema?		شو قولك، منروح عالسينما؟
ma fhimt al su'aal/	I did not understand the question	ما فهمت السؤال
'ala kil Haal bshoufak boukra/ any how, I'll see you tomorrow		على كل حال بشوفك بكرا
mamnoun, saamiHni/	thanks, forgive me	ممنون. سامحني
keef al Taqs 'indak?/how is the weather where you are?		كيف الطقس عندك؟
Jaayyi 'aSfi kbeeri/	a big storm is coming	جايي عاصفة كبيرة
fee talj kteer/	there is a lot of snow	في تلج كتير
al shams ab 'ad min al amar/ the sun is farther than the moon		الشمس ابعد من القمر

al samaa zar'a/	the sky is blue	السما زرقا
fee barq w ra 'd/	there is lightning and thunder	في برق ورعد
Jaayyi mawjit shawb awiyyi/	a strong heat wave is coming	جايي موجة شوب قويي
kim yawm fi bil osbou '/	how many days are in a week?	كم يوم في بالأسبوع؟
kim osbou ' bil shahr?/	how many weeks in a month?	كم اسبوع بالشهر؟
kim shahr bil sini?/	how many months in a year?	كم شهر بالسنة؟
al saa 'a fiiha sitteen dqiqa/	there are 60 minutes in an hour	الساعة فيها ستين دقيقة
laHza min fadhlak/	one moment please	لحظة من فضلك
bshoufak ba 'd al dhuhr/	see you in the afternoon	بشوفك بعد الضهر
iddaysh al saa 'a halla'/	what time is it now?	اديش الساعة هلق؟
shahr aab shawb kteer/	the month of August is very hot	شهر آب شوب كتير
'indu 'ayli kbeeri/	he has a big family	عندو عيلة كبيرة
'ammu SaaHib shirki/	his uncle owns a company	عمو صاحب شركة
khayyu mwadhaf Hkoumi/	his brother is a government employee	خيو موظف حكومي
khaalu mitqaa 'id/	his uncle is retired	خالو متقاعد
martu mudeerit madrasi/	his wife is a school director	مرتو مديرة مدرسة
'ammu mTalliq/	his uncle is divorced	عمو مطلّق
haydi bint yateemi/	this is an orphaned girl	هيدي بنت يتيمة
mshabshib/	he is looking younger	مشبشب
Si 'ru khamsi w 'ishreen dollar/	its price is 25 dollars	سعرو خمسة وعشرين دولار
fataH al baab w 'aal tfadhal/	he opened the door and said please come in	فتح الباب وقال تفضل
bta 'rif tirsum kharTit libnaan/	do you know how to draw the map of Lebanon?	بتعرف ترسم خارطة لبنان
smi 't al akhbaar/	I heard the news	سمعت الأخبار
l 'ibna bil wara'/	we played cards	لعبنا بالورق
tarjam al maktoub bil 'arabi/	he translated the letter into Arabic	ترجَم المكتوب بالعربي

libis tyaabu w raaH ma 'un/ he put his clothes on and went with them	لبس تيابو وراح معن
shalaH tyaabu w naam/ he took off his clothes and went to sleep	شلح تيابو ونام
baddi zour ' amti bukra/ I want to visit my aunt tomorrow	بدي زور عمتي بكرا
baddu yishtri siyyaara jdiidi/ he wants to buy a new car	بدو يشتري سيارة جديدة
laysh t'akhart 'al ijtimaa '/ why were you late to the meeting?	ليش تأخرت عالاجتماع؟
keef bitHib al ahwi/ how do you like the coffee?	كيف بتحب القهوي؟
mjawwaz aw a 'zab/ are you married or single?	مجوّز او أعزب؟
shou arrart ta 'mil/ what did you decide to do?	شو قررت تعمل؟
wayn ktaab al adab/ where is the literature book?	وين كتاب الأدب؟
baytkun b 'eed min hawn/ your house is far from here	بيتكن بعيد من هون
badna nishrab ahwi/ we want to drink coffee	بدنا نشرب قهوي
barki laazim nrouH/ perhaps we should go	بركي لازم نروح
' am idrus halla'/ I am studying now	عم ادرس هلق
ma darast mbaariH/ I did not study yesterday	ما درست مبارح
kint mashghoul/ I was busy	كنت مشغول
saafart 'a fransa/ I travelled to France	سافرت ع فرنسا
ma baddi aakul djaaj/ I do not want to eat chicken	ما بدي آكل دجاج
meelaad majeed w 'aam sa 'eed/ Merry Christmas and Happy New Year	ميلاد مجيد وعام سعيد
ana nabaati/ I am vegetarian	انا نباتي
ana aTwal minnak/ I am taller than you	انا أطول منك
huwwi aTwal minna/ he is taller than us	هوي أطول منا
huwwi 'iraaqi/ he is Iraqi	هوي عراقي
bass, bikaffi/ stop, enough	بس. بكفّي
ma 'u passpor amerkaani/ he has an American passport	معو باسبور أمركاني
shou 'aaSmit al yaman/ what is the capital of Yemen?	شو عاصمة اليمن؟
meen ra'is al jamhouriyyi/ who is the president?	مين رئيس الجمهورية؟

siyyartu lawna azra'/	the color of his car is blue	سيارتو لونا أزرق
amiSou Hamra/	his shirt is red	قميصو حمرا
sha 'ra ashqar/	her hair is blond	شعرا اشقر
kaan mariidh bas Saar aHsan/ he was sick but he became better		كان مريض بس صار أحسن
huwwi bishi ' bas martu Hilwi/ he is ugly but his wife is beautiful		هوي بشع بس مرتو حلوي
mish mumkin rouH ma 'un/ it is impossible for me to go with them		مش ممكن روح معن
mamnou ' al wuqouf/	no stopping here	ممنوع الوقوف
shou aTrash?/	are you deaf?	شو، أطرش؟
mish khaayif minnak/	I am not afraid of you	مش خايف منّك
laysh 'aSabi al yawm/	why are you nervous today?	ليش عصبي اليوم؟
ibnou walad kislaan bil madrasi/ his son is a lazy boy at school		ابنو ولد كسلان بالمدرسة
meen Hadhrit al shab/	who is this young man?	مين حضرة الشب؟
khalleek hawn allayli/	stay here tonight	خليك هون الليلة
ma kaan fee shee baynaatna/ there was nothing between us		ما كان في شي بيناتنا
ma tihtam bil issa/ do not pay attention to the story/ do not worry about it		ما تهتم بالقصة
shou baddak minni/	what do you want with me?	شو بدك مني؟
mish ' ala baali idrus/	I do not feel like studying	مش على بالي ادرس
baytna bil binaayee likbeeri, 'al yameen, bilTaabi' al khaamis/ our house is in the big building, on the right, on the 5th floor		بيتنا بالبناية الكبيرة، عاليمين، بالطابق الخامس
' inna jnayni kbeeri khalf al bayt/ we have a big garden behind the house		عنا جنينة كبيرة خلف البيت
wayn al miftaaH/	where is the key?	وين المفتاح؟
sakkir al birdaayee/	close the curtain	سَكِر البرداية
ftaaH al birraad/	open the fridge	فتاح البراد
waaqif ' al balkon/	standing on the balcony	واقف ع البلكون
baddu mkhaddi taHt raasu/ he wants a pillow under his head		بدو مخدة تحت راسو

Lesson One

MARḤABA مرحبا	HELLO
MARḤABTAYN مرحبتين	HELLO(TWO)
KĪFAK? كيفَك	How are you? M.S.
KĪFIK? كيفِك	How are you? F.S.
IL ḤAMDILLA, KĪFAK INTA? الحمدلله كَيفَك أنتَ	Thank God, how are you? M.S.
IL ḤAMDILLA, -KĪFIK INTI? الحمدلله كيفِك إنتِ	Thank God, how are you? F.S.
MABSūṬ, SHUKRAN مبسوط شكراً	Fine, thanks. M.S.
MABSūṬA, SHUKRAN مبسوطة شكرًا	Fine, thanks. F.S.

Lesson Two

MARḤABA مرحبا	Hello
MARāḤIB مراحب	Hello(S) Plural
KīFAK ILYAWM كيفَك اليوم	How are you today? M.S.
ILYAWM اليوم	Today
ILḤAMDILLA MABSūṬ الحمدلله مبسوط	Thank GOD, fine. M.S
KīFIK ILYAWM? كيفِك اليوم	How are you today? F.S
ILḤAMDILLA, MABS ūṬA الحمدلله، مبسوطة	Thank GOD, fine. F.S
NUSHKUR ALLA نشكر الله	Thank God
MABSūṬA KTīR مبسوطة كتير	Very happy F.S.
KīFAK INTA? كيفَك انتَ	How are you? M.S

NUSHKUR ALLA MABSūṬA KTīR نشكر الله مبسوطة كتير	Thank GOD, Very happy. F.S
ALLA الله	GOD
INTI انتِ	You .F.S.
INT,(INTA) انت	You .M.S
MARḤABA مرحبا	Hello
MARāḤIB مراحب	Hello(S) Plural

PRONUNCIATION DRILL

BAYT بيت	House
BINT بنت	Girl
SHAJARA شجرة	Tree
SHIBBāK شبّاك	Window

KIRSī كرسي	Chair
ṬāWLI طاولي (طاولة)	Table
ḤāYṬ حيط (حائط)	Wall
SAMA سما (سماء)	Sky
SHAMS شمس	Sun
AMAR(QAMAR) أمر (قمر)	Moon
SHABAKI شبكي (شبكة)	Net
HAYDA AMAR هيدا(هذا) أمر(قمر)	This is a moon
HAYDA BāB هيدا باب	This is a door
HAYDA SHIBBāK هيدا شبّاك	This is a window
HAYDA ḤāYṬ هيدا حيط(حائط)	This is a wall
HAYDI BINT هيدي(هذه) بنت	This is a girl

HAYADI SHABAKI هيدي شبكي(شبكة)	This is a net
HAYDI ṬāWLI هيدي طاولي(طاولة)	This is a table
HAYDI KIRSI هيدي كرسي	This is a chair
HAYDI SAMA هيدي سما(سماء)	This is a sky
HAYDI SHAMS هيدي شمس	This is a sun
SHū HAYDA? شو هيدا (ما هذا)	HAYDA(door) BAB
SHū HAYDA?	HAYDA(window)
SHū HAYDA?	HAYDA(house)
SHū HAYDA?	HAYDA(moon)
SHū HAYDA?	HAYDA(wall)
SHū HAYDI? شو هيدي (ما هذه)	HAYDI(SHABAKI)
SHū HAYDI?	HAYDI(table)
SHū HAYDI?	HAYDI(chair)
SHū HAYDI?	HAYDI(sun)

Hayda = هيدا = هذا = This (is) = Used for M. S.
Haydi = هيدي = هذه = This (is) = Used for F.S.
Hawdy = هودي = These (are) = Used for plural, both M & F.

Lesson Three

Sāmi: Marḥaba Samīr Kīfak Ilyawm?

مرحبا سمير كيفَك اليوم

Hello Samīr how are you today?

Samīr: Ilḥamdilla, Mabsūṭ, Kīf Sāmia?

الحمدلله مبسوط كيف سامية

Thank God, fine, how is Sāmia?

Sāmi: Sāmia Mish Hawn Ilyawm, Rāḥit Tzūr Imma

سامية مش هون اليوم، راحت تزور إما(امّها)

Sāmia is not here today. She went to visit her mother

Samīr: Inta Hawn Bukra?

انتَ هون بكرا؟

Are you (going to be) here tomorrow?

Sāmi: Iza Alla rād

(إذا) ازا الله راد

If GOD willed (so)

PRONUNCIATION DRILL

IZA ازا (إذا)	If
ILYAWM اليوم	Today
BUKRA بكرا – بكرة	Tomorrow
KTīR كتير	Very much, Much
MISH مش	Is not
HAWN هون	Here
MISH HAWN مش هون	Is not here.(NOT HERE)
RāḤIT راحت	She went
RāḤ راح	He went
ZYāRA زيارة	Visit
IMMA	Her mother

(امّها) إما	
IMMI إمي	My mother
IMMAK إمك	Your mother (MS)
ḤAYT حيط	Wall
ISM اسم	Name
ISMI اسمي	My name (is)
ISMAK اسمَك	Your name(M.S)
MīN? مين	Who?(is)
MīN INT? مين إنتَ	Who are you
BAYYAK بيّك	Your father(M.S)
BAYYIK بيِّك	Your father(F.S)
BAYYI بيي	My father

Translate into Arabic: ترجم للعربي	tarjim lil 'Arabi
Who is your mother? (F.S): مين امِك؟	meen immik?
How are you Samīr? سمير؟	keefak ya Samir? كيفك يا
Thank God, very happy? : kteer نشكر الله، مبسوط كتير	nushkur allah, mabsouT
What is your name? (M.S):	shou ismak? شو اسمك؟
My name is Samīr:	ismi Samir اسمي سمير
How is your father today? : بيّك اليوم ؟	keef bayyak ilyawm? كيف
Thank God, fine: منيح	ilHamdilla, mneeeH الحمدلله،
This is a wall? :	hayda HayT هيدا حيط
This is a sky? :	haydi sama هيدي سما
This is a chair? :	haydi kirsi هيدي كرسي
This is a table? :	haydi Tawli هيدي طولي

This is a net? :	haydi shabaki
هيدي شبكي	
What is this?	This is a door shou hayda?,
hayda baab هيدا باب شو هيدا؟	
This is a house:	hayda bayt هيدا بيت

Lesson Four

Sāmia: Ṣabāḥ Ilkhair ya Sāmi, Shū ȧamil Ilyawm ?

صباح الخير يا سامي، شو عامل اليوم؟

Good morning Sāmi, what are you doing today?

Sāmi: Ṣabāḥ ilnūr ya Sāmia, Rāyeḥ ȧal sūq Ishtri khudra Lilbayt

صباح النور يا سامية، رايح على السوء(السوق) اشتري خضرة للبيت

Good morning Sāmia, I am going to the market to buy vegetables for the house.

Samīr: Shū 'awlak Iza Ana Ruḫt Maȧak?

شو أولك (قولك) ازا(إذا) انا رحت معك؟

What do you say if I went with you?

Samīra: Fīk tjībli Kīlo BaTaTa Maȧak?

فيك تجبلي كيلو بطاطا معك

Can you bring for me one kilo of potatoes with you?

Samīr: Tikramī yā Sāmia.

You are welcome, Sāmia.

تكرمي يا سامية

Sāmia: Shukran Ktīr ya Samīr.

Thanks a lot, Samīr.

شكراً كتير يا سمير

Sāmia: Ana Baddi Tlāti Kīlo Laymūn.

انا بدي تلاته كيلو ليمون

I want three kilos of oranges.

Sāmi: Tikramī, Baddik Shī Baʿad?

تكرمي، بدك شي بعد؟

You are welcome. Do you want anything else?

Sāmia: la. Shoukran ya Samir

لا. شكرا يا سامي.

No. Thanks a lot, Samī.

PRONUNCIATION DRILL

BATāTA بطاطا	Potatoes
BAṣAL بصل	Onions
BAYḌ بيض	Eggs

MILḤ ملح	Salt
SUKKAR سكّر	Sugar
BADDI بدّي	I want(to)
DIBB دبّ	Bear
SHAB شب	A young man
KTāB كتاب	Book
DAFTAR دفتر	Notebook
KALB كلب	Dog
BSAYNI بسيني (قطة)	Cat
SHāB شاب	He grew white hair
KABAS كَبَس	He pressed
SAKAN سَكن	He resided
BIKI	He cried

بكي (بكى)	
KIMM كِم	Sleeve
KīS كيس	Bag
SIKKīN(I) سكينة	Knife
FALLINI فلينة	Cork
DIKKāN(I) دكان	Small Shop
ALAM الم (قلم)	Pen-Pencil
ʾIID إيد (يد)	Hand
RāS راس (رأس)	Head
MAKTAB مكتب	Office

Translate into Arabic	tarjim lil ʻArabi
ترجم للعربي	
This is a cat: هيدي بسيني	haydi bsayni

My name is Sāmi:	ismi Sami	اسمي سامي
Sāmia is not here:	Samia mish hawn	ساميا مش هون
You are welcome:	ahla w sahla	اهلا وسهلا
Thanks a lot:	shoukran kteer	شكرا كتير
Do you want anything else?	baddak shee ghayrou?	بدك شي غيرو؟
Do you want eggs?	baddik baydh?	بدك بيض؟
Good morning Sāmia:	SabaaH alkhayr ya Samia	صباح الخير يا ساميا
I am going to the market:	ana raayeH 'al souq	انا رايح عالسوق
I am not here today:	ana mish hawn ilyawm	انا مش هون اليوم
Be here tomorrow:	koun hawn bukra	كون هون بكرا
If God willed:	iza Alla raad	ازا الله راد
Thanks a lot:	shoukran kteer	شكرا كتير

What is your name?	shou ismak?	شو اسمك؟
Who is your father?	meen bayyak?	مين بيّك؟
My mother is not here:	immi mish hawn	امي مش هون
She went to visit her mother:	raaHit tzour imam	راحت تزور اما
Who are you?	meen int?	مين انت؟
This is a chair:	haydi kirsi	هيدي كرسي
This is a table:	haydi Tawli	هيدي طولي

Lesson Five

Kamāl: Mbāriḥ Istalamt Maktūb

إمبارح إستلمت مكتوب

Yesterday I received a letter.

Sāmia: Min Miin?

من مين؟

From whom?

Kamāl: Min Ṣāḫbi Bi- Fransa

من صاحبي بفرنسا

From my friend in France.

Sāmia: Shū Khabbarak?

شو خبّرك؟

What did he tell you?

Kamāl: Khabbarni Innū 'Am yidrus Ṭubb

خبرني انّو عم يدرس طب

He told me that he is studying medicine.

Sāmia: Ana Fakkart Innū Kan 'Am yidrus Adab

انا فكرت انو كان عم يدرس أدب

I thought that he was studying literature.

Kamāl: Lā, Khayyu Daras Adab Mish Huwwi

لأ. خيو درس ادب مش هوّي

No, his brother studied literature, not him.

Sāmia: Shū Darasit Ikhtu?

شو درست اختو؟

What did his sister study?

Kamāl: Ikhtu Darasit Tārīkh

اختو درست تاريخ

His sister studied History.

PRONUNCIATION DRILL

BADDI	I want
بدّي	
āKUL	Eat
آكل	
ISHRAB	Drink
إِشرب	
Nām	Sleep
نام	
IDRUS	Study
إِدرس	
IL ʿAB	Play
إِلعب	

IMSHI إمشي	Walk
RūḤ روح	Go
IJI إجي	Come (to)
IJIT إجت	She arrived
ISTāZ استاز (استاذ)	Teacher
TILMīZ تلميز (تلميذ)	Student
JāM'A جامعة	University
MADRASI مدرسة	School
MKHADDI مخدي (مخدة)	Pillow
MARA مرا (امرأة)	Woman
RIĪJāL رجّال (رجل)	Man
IBNI ابني	My son

BINTI بنتي (ابنتي)	My Daughter
TAKHT تخت	Bed
SHāRI' شارع	Street

Translate into Arabic: ترجم للعربي	tarjim lil ' arabi
I want to drink: اشرب	baddi ishrab بدي
This is a University: هيدي جامعة	haydi jaam 'a
She arrived today: هيي وصلت اليوم	hiyyi wiSlit al yawm
This is a man: رجال	hayda rijjaal هيدا
My son is here: هون	ibni hawn ابني
This is a bed: تخت	hayda takht هيدا
I want to walk: بدي امشي	baddi imshi
I want to study Literature: بدي ادرس ادب	baddi idrus adab

She studied History: هيي درست تاريخ	hiyyi darasit taarikh
She went to the market: راحت عالسوق	raaHit ʿal souq
What do you say if I went with you? ʿik? شو قولك ازا رحت معك؟	shou awlik iza riHt ma
I want sugar, salt and oranges: laymoun بدي سكر، ملح وليمون	baddi sukkar, milH, w
He told me that: هوِي خبرني	huwwi khabbarni
His brother studied medicine: خيو درس طب	khayyu daras Tubb
Yesterday I received a letter مبارح استلمت رسالة	mbaariH istalamt risaali

انا = I- am	Ana =
انتَ You M.S.	Inta =
انتِ = You F.S.	Inti =
هوي= He	Huwi =
هيي= She	Hiyyi =
هني = They two M. & F.	Hinny =

انتو = **You Plural M. & F.**	**Intu =**
نحن = **We**	**Nihna =**
هني = **They plural M. & F.**	**Hinni =**

Lesson Six

Sāmi: Mama, ana juʿaan Ktīr

ماما انا (جوعان)كثير

Mom, I am very hungry.

Mama: yalla, il'akl Ḥāḍir

يللا الأكل حاضر

Come on, the food is ready.

Sāmi: Shū ṭabakhti ilyawm?

شو طبختي اليوم

What did you cook today?

Mama: ṭabakht Djaaj maʿ ruz

طبخت دجاج مع رز

I cooked chicken with rice

Sāmi: Bas?

بس

Is that all? Only?

Mama: La, Kamān Iʿmilit tabbūli wkibbi Nayyi

لا. كمان عملت تبولة وكبة نبّة

No, I also made tabbūli and kibbi Nayyi (raw Kibbi)

Sāmi: ʿaziim, ana ʿazamt ṣāḥbī ta-yākul maʿi

عظيم أنا عزمت صاحبي تياكل معي

Great , I invited my friend to eat with me.

PRONUNCIATION DRILL

LAYSH ليش	Why?
FAKK فك	He undid
FAYY فَي (ظل)	shade
FANN فَن	art
NAKAR نكر	He denied
HAWNīK هونيك	There
SAMM سَم	Poison
SIRR سر	secret
BAWSI بوسي	Kiss
SAWA سوا	together
INTU انتو (انتم)	You. p. M & F

NIḤNA نحنا (نحن)	We (are) P.M.& F
MAAZA مازة (مقبلات)	appetizer
TIMM تم (فم)	mouth
SHAʿR شَعر	hair
ʿAYN عين	eye
ANF أنف	Nose

Translate into Arabic:	tarjim lil 'arabi	ترجم للعربي
I want a kiss:	baddi bawsi	بدي بوسي
This is a secret:	hayda sirr	هيدا سرّ
We are here today:	niHna hawn al yawm	نحن هون اليوم
We are not here tomorrow:	niHna mish hawn bukra	نحن مش هون بكرا
I want Maaza:	baddi maaza	بدّي مازا

He undid the net:	fakk al shabaki	فكّ الشبكة
I want to study Art:	baddi idrus fann	بدي ادرس فن
The house(is) there:	albayt hawneek	البيت هونيك
Why did you go to the market?	laysh riHt ʿ al souq?	ليش رحت عالسوق؟
Are you ready?	int Haadhir?	انت حاضر؟
I want potatoes with rice:	baddi baTaTa maʿ roz	بدّي بطاطا مع رز
My friend wants to eat with me:	SaaHbi baddou yaakul maʿi	صاحبي بدو ياكل معي
She did not have time to cook	ma kaan ʿinda waqt tuTboukh	ما كان عندا وقت تطبخ
He is a great cook	huwwi Tabbaakh ʿazeem	هوي طباخ عظيم
]fried fish and grilled chicken	Samak miʾli w djaaj mishwi	سمك مقلي ودجاج مشوي

Lesson Seven

Sāmi: wayn Kint mbārih?

وين كنت مبارح

Where were you yesterday?

Salaḥ: Kint Bijjāmˁa

كنت بالجامعة

I was at the university.

Sāmi: Jīt lazurak Baˁd ilduhur

جيت لزورك بعد الظهر

I came to visit you in the afternoon.

Salaḥ: mit'assif, Kān ˁindi imtiḥān Jighrāfia

متأسف كان عندي امتحان جغرافيا

I am sorry, I had an exam in Geography.

Sāmi: Kīf Iʿmilt?

كيف عملت

How did you do?

Salaḥ: La bās, kān Lāzim ʿamil aḥsan

لابأس. كان لازم اعمل احسن

Not bad, I should have done better.

PRONUNCIATION DRILL

RASH رش	To spray
SHWāRIB (شارب) شوارب	moustache
ḌIḤIK ضحك	He laughed
HARAB هرب	He ran away, escape
LIBIS لبس	He dressed up

موسيقى

MASRAHIYYI مسرحية	play
MUSI'A موسيقى	music
ṢūRA صورة	picture
MUṭRIB مطرب	singer

Translate into Arabic: tarjim lil 'arabi	ترجم للعربي
I was at the market yesterday: mbaariH	kint bil souq كنت بالسوق مبارح
I cooked chicken with rice: roz	Tabakht djaaj ma ' طبخت دجاج ورز
I came to visit you in the morning:	jeet zoorak 'abukra جيت زورك عبكرة
Sorry, Samia is not here today: hawn al yawm ساميا مش هون اليوم	mit'assif, Samia mish متأسف.
I had an exam in Literature: adab كان عندي امتحان ادب	kaan 'indi imtiHaan
How did you do?:	keef I 'milt? كيف عملت؟
Sami laughed yesterday:	Sami diHik mbaariH سامي ضحك مبارح
This is a picture:	haydi Soura هيدي صورة
Music and singer: muTrib	mousiqa w موسيقى ومطرب

Lesson Eight

Hishām: Ilyawm mish bard

اليوم مش برد

Today is not cold.

Maha: La, mish shawb (Ḥar) w mish bard

لا اليوم مش شوب(حار) ومش برد

No, not hot, and not cold

Hishām: Bitrūḥi mishwār maʿi

بتروحي مشوار معي

Would you go for a walk with me?

Maha: lawyn?

لوين(الى اين)

Where?

Hishām: nimshiʿashaT ilbaḥr

نمشي عَشط(على شاطئ) البحر

To walk by the sea-shor.e

Maha: Balki shattit (Maṭarit)

بلكي شتت (مطرت)

Suppose (perhaps) it rained

Hishām: bitkhāfi min ish shiti?

بتخافي من الشتي(الشتاء)

Are you afraid of the rain?

Maha: La, bkhaaf min ilra'd

لا. بخاف من الرعد

No, I am afraid of thunder.

Hishām: ma tkhāfi

ما تخافي

Do not be afraid

Construct three separate sentences in Arabic, not less than six words each. Use any vocabulary you already know.

Conjugate the verbs: mishi مشي – khaf خاف with all pronouns.

Sample conjugation of the verb (to see) (saw) شاف shaaf:		
أنا شفتْ = saw	ana shift =	I
انتَ شفتْ = You M.S. saw	inta shift =	
انتِ شفتي = You F.S. saw	inti shifti =	

هوي شاف = He saw	huwi shaaf =
هيي شافتْ = She saw	hiyyi shaafit =
هني شافو = They two M. & F. saw	hinny shaafu =
انتو شفتو = You Plural M. & F. saw	intu shiftu =
نحن شفنا = We saw	nihna shifna =
هني شافو = They plural M. & F. saw	hinni shaafu =

PRONUNCIATION DRILL

SHAAF شاف	He saw
SHAM شم	He smelled
SIMI ٘ سمع	He heard
SAMAK سمك	fish
MIFTAAH̲ مفتاح	Key
SHAWWAB	He felt Hot

شوّب	
BARAD برد	He felt cold
NI‘IS نعِس	He felt sleepy
HAWA هوا (رياح)	Wind/ Air
MA BADDI ما بدي	I do not want

Translate into Arabic: tarjim lil ‘ arabi ترجم للعربي	
I do not want to go with you: ما بدّي روح معك	ma baddi rouH ma ‘ak
He saw the moon: هوي شاف القمر	huwi shaaf al amar
He smelled the onions: هوي شمّ البصل	huwi sham al baSal
The key is with me: المفتاح معي	al miftaaH ma ‘I
I want to eat fish, rice, and chicken: بدّي آكل سمك، رز، ودجاج djaaj	baddi aakul samak, roz, w
Do not be afraid: ma tkhaaf	ما تخاف
Today is cold: al yawm bard	اليوم برد
Walk in the street: imshi bil shaari ‘	امشي بالشارع

Do not be afraid of the mayh test:	ma tkhaaf min imtiHaan al Hisaab	ما تخاف من امتحان الحساب
Suppose I am hungry:	balki ana ju 'aan	بلكي انا جوعان
I called the lawyer	talfant lil muhami	تلفنت للمحامي
Why are you sad	laysh zi ' laan	ليش زعلان
Do not blame me	ma tloumni	ما تلومني
Foreigners are not allowed	mamnou ' dukhoul al ajaanib	ممنوع دخول الأجانب
He must have an operation	laazim ya ' mil 'amaliyyi	لازم يعمل عملية
We do not want anyone to know	maa badna Hada ya 'rif	ما بدنا حدا يعرف
I told you not to go	iltillak ma trouH	التلك ما تروح
He won the lottery	ribiH bil yanaaSeeb	ربح ب اليانصيب
He has a dog and a cat	'indu kalb wi bsayni	عندو كلب وبسينة
I am sick and cannot come	ana mareedh ma fiyyee ijee	انا مريض ما فيي اجي
Do not forget the medicine	maa tinsa l dawaa	ما تنسى الدواء
He is in love with her	huwwi maghroum fiha	هوي مغروم فيها
Love is blind	il Hubb a 'ma	الحب اعمى

Lesson Nine

Hishām: lawayn rāyiḫ ya Sāmi?

لوين رايح يا سامي

Where are you going? Sāmi

Sāmi: rāyiḥ 'al maktabi idrus, w'inta?

رايح عَ المكتبة ادرس، وانتَ

I am going to the library to study, and you?

Hishām: Ana rāyiḥ iḫdar sinama

انا رايح احضر سينما

I am going to see a movie.

Sāmi: Laḫālak? Waḫdak?

لحالك، وحدك

Alone? Alone?

Hishām: yemkin ṣāḥbi yrūḥ ma'i

يمكن صاحبي يروح معي

Maybe my friend will come with me.

Sāmi: mīn ṣāḥbak?

مين صاحبك؟

Who is your friend?

Hishām: Ṣāḥbi jāyyi zyāra lamiddit shahr min Bayrūt.

صاحبي جاي زيارة لمدة شهر من بيروت

My friend is coming for a one month visit from Beirut.

Sāmi: Shū 'ismu?

شو اسمو

What is his name?

Hishām: 'ismu Farīd.

His name is Farīd

اسمو فريد

Sāmi: Shū Bya'mil?

شو بيعمل

What does he do?

Hishām: Huwwi tilmīz Bil jām'a L-Libnaniyi

هوي تلميذ بالجامعة اللبنانية

He is a student in the Lebanese university.

سنة - سنين

PRONUNCIATION DRILL

TLAMIIZ تلاميز	students
A' LāM (أقلام) ألالام	Pens
DAFāTIR دفاتر	Note Books
KUTUB كتب	Books
ABWāB أبواب	doors
FāTIT (دخلت) فاتت	She entered
ḤīṬāN حيطان	walls
MADRASI مدرسة	School
MADāRIS مدارس	Schools

باب

حيط
HayT

TALLI (تلّة) تلّي	Hill
TLāL تلال	Hills
TīN تين	Figs
ʿINAB عنب	Grapes
SHBāBīK شبابيك	windows
MAWZ موز	banana
KARāSI كراسي	Chairs

Translate into Arabic:	tarjim lil ʿarabi ترجم للعربي
I am going to see a play:	raayiH shouf/ iHdhar masraHiyyi رايح شوف ــ احضر مسرحيّة
She is a student at the university:	hiyyi Taalbi bil jam ʿa هيي طالبة بالجامعة
This is a pen:	hayda alam هيدا قلم
What did you cook today?:	shou Tabakhti al yawm شو طبختِ اليوم؟

She entered the house alone: waHda	faatit 'al bayt فاتت عالبيت وحدا
He is a student at the school: madrasi	huwi tilmeez bil هوي تلميز بالمدرسة
I want to eat figs:	baddi aakul teen بدّي آكل تين
He is coming to visit for a month: shahr	jaayi zyaara lamiddit جايي زيارة لمدة شهر
My friend is a teacher:	SaaHbi istaaz صاحبي استاز
Where did Samia go?:	wayn raaHit Samia? وين راحت ساميا؟
Did you go alone?: laHaalak?	riHt waHdak? رحت وحدك؟ لحالك؟

مدة = period duration = for duration X

مدة = J + ـ ة

Lesson Ten

Say the following in Arabic: بالعربي	oul/ qoul bil 'arabi: قول
1. What is this? (M. F شو هيدا؟ شو هيدي؟	shou hayda/ shou haydi?
2. What are these?	Shou hawdi? شو هودي؟
3. Who are you? (M. F) انتَ؟ مين انتِ؟	meen inta/ meen inti? مين
4. This is a school?	haydi madrasi هيدي مدرسة
5. This is a book.	hayda ktaab هيدا كتاب
6. These are schools.	hawdi madaaris هودي مدارس
7. What does he do? biyishtighil? شو بيعمل؟ شو بيشتغل؟	shou biya 'mil/
8. I want to eat.	baddi aakul بدي آكل
9. Where are you going? (M.F) رايح؟ رايحا؟	wayn raayiH/ raayHa? وين
10. What do you want to hear? بدك تسمع؟	shou baddak tisma ' شو
11. Where is your mother?	Wayn immak? وين امك؟
12. I am going to see a movie? رايح شوف، احضر، سينما cinama	raayiH shouf/ iHdhar
13. He is a student in the Lebanese university? huwi	

	Taalib bil jaam 'a il libnaaniyyi	هو طالب بالجامعة اللبنانية
14.	I do not want to study with you. ما بدي ادرس معك	ma baddi idrus ma 'ak
15.	She is cold. هيي برداني	hiyyi birdaani
16.	Whose book is this? كتاب مين هيدا؟	ktaab meen hayda?
17.	Where were you yesterday? وين كنت مبارح؟	Wayn kint mbaariH?
18.	I came to visit you. زورك	jeet zourak جيت
19.	I do not know his name. ما بعرف اسما	maa ba 'rif ismaa
20.	What did you hear on the news? شو سمعت ب الأخبار ؟	Shou smi 't bil akhbaar?
21.	She went to the dentist. راحت لعند حكيم الاسنان	raaHit la 'ind Hakeem l snaan
22.	I want a table near the window. بدي طولي حد الشباك	baddi Tawlee Had l shibbaak

Lesson Eleven

Mbāriḥ riḥna maʿ jīrānnā tānzur ʿamtī bil-mistashfa. ʾAltarīʾwa
ʾafna-l-polīs waʿatānā zabt. Jārna Samīr ziʿil ktīr w ʾarrar
yirjaʿ. Lamma wsilnā Kān fi nās ktīr Nāṭrīn yzūrū ʾarāyibhun
Hawnīk. Issāʿa tnāʿsh samaḥ-l-ḥakīm innū nshūf

ʿamti. Fitna - w-kānit –l- ghurfi nḍīfi ktīr, w-ʿamti ʿam tiḍḥak.
IʿRifnā innū fiyā titruk yawm -l-ʾurbaʿa-l-jāyi. Inbasaṭnā
ktīr, wil-mama bikyit min il faraḥ.

Lammā rijiʿnā wisil bayyi minil shighl.

Saʾalnā wayn Kinnā. Immi Haḍḍarit-L-ʿasha. W-kil-l-ʿayli
Akalit sawa.

جاره / جار ج جيران neighbor

Jaara

مبارح رحنا مع جيرانا تتزور عمتي بالمستشفى. على الطريق وقفنا البوليس وأعطانا

ضبط، جارنا سمير زعل كتير وقرر يرجع. لما وصلنا كان في ناس كتير ناطرين

يزوروا ارايبهن هونيك.

الساعة تناعش سمح الحكيم انو نشوف عمتي. فتنا وكانت الغرفة نظيفة كتير،

وعمتي عم تضحك. عرفنا انو فيها تترك يوم الاربعا الجاي. انبسطنا كتير، والماما

بكت من الفرح. لما رجعنا وصل بيي من الشغل. سألنا وين كنا. إمي حضرت

العشا، وكل العيلي اكلت سوا.

Yesterday we went with our neighbors to visit my (paternal) aunt in the hospital. On the way, the police stopped us and gave us a ticket. Our neighbor Samir was very sad and he decided to go back. When we arrived (at the hospital), there were many people waiting to visit their relatives there.

At 12 o'clock the Doctor allowed us to see my aunt. We entered and her room was very clean. My aunt was laughing. We learned that she can leave next Wednesday. We were very happy and my mother cried with joy. When we returned, my dad had just arrived from work. He asked where we were. My mother prepared dinner, and the whole family ate together.

مفردات الدرس	Lesson vocabulary	mufradaat al dars	
وقفنا	wa'afnaa =	he stopped us	
عطانا	'aTaanaa =	he gave us	
زبط	zabT =	ticket	
زعل	zi 'il =	he became sad	
ناطرين	naaTreen =	they were waiting	
سمح	samaH =	he allowed	
مبارح	mbaariH =	yesterday	
جيرانا	Jiraanna =	our neighbors	
عمتيt	'Amti =	my paternal aun	
مستشفى	mistashfa =	hospital	
زبط	zabt =	ticket	
ارايب	araayib =	relatives	
حكيم	Hakeem =	doctor	
غرفة	ghirfi =	room	
بكت	bikit =	she cried	
عيلي	'ayli =	family	

1. Recite the 12 months of the year in order.

2. Say the days of the week in Arabic. Also, say the numbers from 20-40.

١

Lesson Twelve

Baʿd shahr w-nus bit-ballish furṣit ʿīd l-milād. ʾAna nāṭir l-furṣa ḥatta itruk l-jāmʿa wil-kitub wil dars w-rūḥ ʿalbayt shuf ahlī w-aṣḥābi. Baytna bʿīd miit mīl min hawn. Ana maʿ indi siyyāra. Yemkin rūḥ bil-train. Bas bil-ṭiyyāra ktīr ghāly. Ma fiyyi idfaʿ ḥaʾl-biṭāʾa. Abl ma rūḥ, laazim khallis kil imtiḥanāti. Bit ammal innū injaḥ Ḥatta tkūn l-furṣa hilwi.

Mishtāʾ ʾshūf ahli. Sārli tlāt shhūr ma shiftun. Kil jimʿa kint iktub maktūb la-immi, aw talfin w-iḥki maʿ bayyi w maʿ ikhti. Ana waḥdi hawn, bas lāzim idrus w-itkharraj ākhir l-sini.

بعد شهر ونص بتبلش فرصة عيد الميلاد. انا ناطر الفرصة حتى اترك الجامعة والكتب والدرس وروح ع البيت شوف اهلي واصحابي. بيتنا بعيد ميت ميل من هون. انا ما عندي سيارة، يمكن روح بالتران. بس بالطيارة كتير غالي ما فيي ادفع حأ (حق) البطاقة. ابل (قبل) ما روح لازم خلص كل امتحاناتي. بتأمل انو انجح حتى تكون الفرصة حلوي. مشتاء (مشتاق) شوف أهلي. صارلي تلات شهور ما شفْتن، كل جمعة كنت اكتب مكتوب لأمي، او تلفن واحكي مع بيي ومع اختي. انا وحدي هون، بس لازم ادرس واتخرج آخر السنة.

176

In a month and a half from now Christmas break will start. I am waiting for the break so I can leave the university and the books and my studies and go home to see my family and friends. Our house is a 100 miles away from here. I do not have a car, and may go home by train. But going by plane is very expensive and I cannot pay for the ticket. Before I go, I must finish all my exams. I hope to pass so the break will be enjoyable. I am anxious to see my family. I have not seen them in three months. Every week, I used to write a letter to my mother, or call and talk with my father and my sister. I am alone here, but I must study and graduate by the end of the year.

مفردات الدرس	Lesson vocabulary	mufradaat al dars
نص	half	Nus
ناطر	waiting for	naaTir
ترك	left	tarak
بلّش	began	Ballash
فرصة	break – vacation	FurSa
عيد الميلاد	Christmas	'id 'l miilaad
غالي	expensive	Ghali
ادفع	to pay	Idfa '
جمعة	week	Jim 'a

مكتوب	letter	Maktoub
وحدي	alone	WaHdi
اتخرّج	to graduate	Itkharraj
طيّارة	airplane	Tiyyara
بطاقة	ticket	biTaa'a

Based on the text, answer these questions in Arabic:	
1. When will the break start?	Ba 'd shahr w nuss
2. How far is my home?	meeyet meel
3. How will I go home?	yemkin bil traan
4. What kind of car do I have?	Ma 'indi siyyaara
5. How long have I been away from home?	tlaat shhour
6. What is my sister's name?	mish ma 'rouf

1. Use 5 vocabulary words, each in a separate sentence.

2. Conjugate the verb (to wait) in the past with all pronouns.

انا ana naTart =	I waited	انا نطرتْ
انتَ = inta naTart =	You M.S.	انتَ نطرتْ
انتِ = inti naTarti =	You F.S.	انتِ نطرتِ
هوي = huwi naTar =	He	هوي نطر
هيي = hiyyi naTarit =	She	هيي نطرت
هني = hinny naTaru =	They two M. & F.	هني نطرو
انتو = intu naTartu =	You Plural M. & F.	انتو نطرتو
نحن = niHna naTarna =	We	نحن نطرنا
هني = hinni naTaru =	They plural M. & F	هني نطرو

Lesson Thirteen

Saʾalitnī marti iza ʾirīt l-Jarīdi l-yawm.

Jāwabtā: Bas laysh saʾaltī?

Li'annū bint Jārna ṣūritha bil-Jarīdi. Shahr l-jāyi badda titjawwaz. Wil-ʿurs bi-knīsit l-sayidi. Wil ʾarīs shab mumtaaz min ʿayli mnīḥa. Daras handasi madaniyi w-farash bayt ḫilu ktīr bil- jabal Ḫatta yʾaddū l-ṣayfiyi. L-ʿarūs baʿda bil-madrasi. ʿUmra wāHad wʿishrīn, sini bas. Shaʿrha aswad ṭawīl. ʿYūna khudr kbaar. Tawīli w-jismha rafīʿ. Ahlha raḥ yaʿmlu ʾurs kbīr w- yʾzimu nās ktīr min kil- l- Diyaʿ.

سألتتني مرتي اذا اريت (قرأت) الجريدة اليوم، جاوبتها:

بس ليش سألتي؟

لانو بنت جيرانا صورتها بالجريدة. شهر الجاي بدا تتزوج، والعرس بكنيسة السيدة.
والعريس شب ممتاز من عيلة منيحة. درس هندسي مدنيه وفرش بيت حلو كتير
بالجبل حتى يأضو الصيفية. العروس بعدا بالمدرسة. عمرا واحد وعشرين سنة بس،
شعرها اسود طويل وعيونا خضر كبار. طويلي وجسمها رفيع. أهلها رح يعملوا عرس
كبير ويعزموا ناس من كل الضيع.

My wife asked me if I read the newspaper today. I answered:

But, why did you ask?

Because the picture of our neighbors' daughter is in the paper today. Next month she wants to get married and the wedding is in the Church of Our Lady. The groom is an excellent young man from a good family. He studied civil engineering and he furnished a very beautiful house in the mountain so they can spend their summer there. The bride is still in school .She is only 21 years old. Her hair is long and black and her eyes are green and large. She is tall and her body is thin. Her parents are going to have a big wedding and invite people from all the villages.

شعر	Sha 'r =	hair
طويل	Taweel =	long
خضر	Khudr =	green
كبير	Kbeer =	big
عرس	'Urs =	wedding
ناس	Naas =	people
جسم	Jism =	body
ضيع	Diya ' =	villages
جريدة	Jareedi =	newspaper
كنيسة	Kneesi =	church
اسود	Aswad =	black

1. **Talk about a wedding that you attended.**

2. **Say the numbers from 20-40 in Arabic.**

3. **Write down the twelve months of the year.**

4. **Use five vocabulary words, each in a complete sentence.**

Lesson Fourteen

Baʿd l-ʿurs Kān fi ḥaflit istiʾbāl bil otail. Kil L-madʿuwwīn iju. Akalū w-shirbū w-raʾasū. L-ʿarīs wil-ʿarūs rāḥu ʿa-shahr l-ʿasal

lawayn rāḥū?

Ma baʿrif. Yemkin ʾa-ʾītālia, aw-Faransa, aw- Amrica. Ana rjiʿt ʾal- bayt liʾannū Kān ʿindi mawʿid maʿ raʾīs l-shirki maṭraḥ ma bishtghil. Ijtamaʿnā la middit

sāʿtayn. Immi saʾalitnī kīf kān l-ijtimāʿ. ʾIltilla tiʿ bān baʿdayn bkhabrik. Nimt shway w-lamma wʿīt Kint mirtāḥ. Shribt ʾahwi w-talfant lil-khiyyāṭ tayā-khud ʾyāsi w-yaʿ milli badli Jdiīdi lil-shighil.

بعد العرس كان في حفلة استئبال(استقبال) بالاوتيل. كل المدعوين اجوا، اكلوا وشربوا ورأصوا (رقصوا). العريس والعروس راحوا عا شهر العسل. لوين راحو؟ ما بعرف، يمكن على ايطاليا او فرنسا، او امريكا. انا رجعت عَ البيت لانو كان عندي موعد مع رئيس الشركة مطرح ما بشتغل. اجتمعنا لمدة ساعتين. إمي سالتني كيف كان الاجتماع؟ التلا(قلت لها) تعبان بعدين بخبرك. نمت شوي ولما وعيت كنت مرتاح. شربت اهوة (قهوة) وتلفنت للخياط تياخذ اياسي(قياسي) ويعملّي بدلة (بذلة) جديدة للشغل.

مُطرَح
مُطرَح place, postion, locate
onleg here
Seat

مرتاح
مرتاح
مرتاح
مرتاح

/183

After the wedding there was a reception party at the hotel. All the invitees came. They ate, drank and danced. The groom and the bride went on their honeymoon. Where did they go? I do not know. Maybe to Italy, France or America. I returned home because I had an appointment with the president of the company where I work. We met for the period of two hours. My mother asked me how was the meeting? I told her I am tired and will tell you later. I slept a little and when I woke up I was rested. I drank coffee and called the tailor to take my measurements and make me a new suit for work.

Lesson vocabulary	mufradaat al dars	مفردات الدرس
عرس	wedding	'urs
حفلة	party	Hafli
استقبال	reception	Isti'baal
موعد	appointment	maw 'id
مدعوين	invitees	mad 'ueen
شهر	month	shahr
عسل	honey	'asal
بدلة	suit	badlee

لد ل ۸

خِياط
خِياط

خياط	**tailor**	**khiyyaaT**
شركة	**company**	**shirki**
اجتماع	**meeting**	**Ijtimaa '**
تعبان	**tired**	**Ti 'baan**
told – to tell	خبّر	**khabbar**

Based on the text, answer these questions in Arabic:	
What happened after the wedding?	Kaan fee Haflit isti'baal
Why did I call the tailor?	tayaakhud iyaasi
Who attended the wedding?	kil al mad 'uween
Why did I return home? liannu kaan 'indi maw 'id ma ' ra'iis al shirki	
How long was the meeting?	saa 'tayn
What did I do before I called the tailor?	nimt shwayy
Where was the honey moon?	ma ba 'rif

185

Lesson Fifteen

Libnān jumhūriyyi mist' illi. Akhad isti'lālū sint l-'alf w tis'miyyi w-tlāta w –arb'in min Fransa. Ra'īs l- jumhūriyyi dāyman masīḥī. Byintikhbū l-nuwwāb. Majlis l-nuwwāb m'allaf min 128 'uḍu mislim w masīḥī. Byintikhibhum l-sha'b. Ra'is l-majlis dāyman bīkūn mislim shī'I, lākin ra'īs l-wizāra mislim sinni. 'Abl l- ḥarb l-'akhīra kān Libnān mizdihir iqtisādiyyan w-mā fi far' bayn l-masīḥī wil- mislim abadan. Ḥatta yirja' Libnān 'awi, lāzim yittifi' sha' bu w-ya'rfu innū l-dīn lil-lāh wil-waṭan lil-jamī'.

1943

لبنان جمهورية مستئله (مستقلة). اخذ استئلاله(استقلاله) سنة الألف وتسع مئة وتلاتة واربعين من فرنسا. رئيس الجمهورية دايمن(دائماً) مسيحي. بينتخبوا النواب.

مجلس النواب مؤلف من 128 عضو. مسلم ومسيحي بينتخبهم الشعب. رئيس المجلس دايمن بيكون مسلم شيعي، لكن رئيس الوزارة مسلم سني. أبل(قبل) الحرب الأخيرة كان لبنان مزدهر اقتصادياً وما في فرق بين المسيحي والمسلم أبداً. حتى يرجع لبنان أوي (قوي) ، لازم يتفيء(يتفق) شعبو ويعرفوا إنو الدين لله والوطن للجميع.

Bawdhoo

Lebanon is an independent Republic. It earned its independence in the year 1943 from France. The President of the Republic is always a Christian, elected by the members of the Parliament. The Parliament is composed of 128 members; there are Christians and Moslems elected by the people. The Speaker of the House is always a Shi 'a Moslem, but the Prime Minister is a Sunni Moslem. Before the recent war, Lebanon was prosperous economically and there was no distinction between a Moslem and a Christian citizen. In order for Lebanon to return to its previous strength, its people must unite and learn that religion belongs to God and the country belongs to all its citizens.

jumhuriyyi =	republic	جمهورية
isti'laal =	independence	استقلال
ra'iis =	president	رئيس
daayman =	always	دايما
masiiHi =	christian	مسيحي
mislim =	muslim	مسلم
wizaara =	government _ministry_	وزارة
awi =	strong	قوي
mizdihir =	prosperous	مزدهر
waTan =	homeland	وطن
Jamii ' =	all	جميع
iqtiSaad =	economy	اقتصاد
far' =	difference	فرق
Harb =	war	حرب
Wizaara =	ministry	وزارة

Lesson Sixteen

Libnān balad zghīr. Masāḥtuʿashr talāf w-arbaʿ miye witnaīn w khamsīn kilomitr mrabbaʿ. Mashhūr innū balad siyāḥi. Manākhu mumtāz. Biṣaddir fawāki w –khuḍra w-mây maʿ daniyyi. ʿadad sikkānu khams mlāyīn bas. Libnān mish balad ṣināʿi li'annū mā fī masāniʿ kbīri. Il-libnāniyyi biHibbu ysāfru la-oroppa wla amerca. L-yawm bi-sāfruʿal dual l-ʿarabiyyi li'annū fi shighl ktīr. Fi-bi-Libnān arbaʿ jāmʿāt kbār. L-libnāniyyi, l-amerkiyyi, l-ʿarabiyyi wil-yasūʿiyyi. Kil ahl Libnān byaʿrfu yi'ru w-yiktbu. W-muʿzamhun byiḥku frinsāwi w-inglīzi. Ilyawm fi- bi- Libnān Arbaʿa –w- tlātīn Jāmʿa muʿtaraf fīha.

لبنان بلد صغيّر. مساحتو (مساحته) عشر تلاف واربعمية وتنين وخمسين كيلو متر

مربع. مشهور انو بلد سياحي، مناخو (مناخه) معتدل، بصدّر فواكي (فواكه) ومي

moderate

(مياه) معدنية. عدد سكانو (سكانه) خمس ملايين بس. لبنان مش بلد صناعي لأنه

ما في مصانع كبيرة إللبناني (اللبنانيين) بحبوا يسافروا لأوروبا ولأمريكا. اليوم

بيسافروا ع الدول العربية لأنو (لأنه) في شغل كتير. في بلبنان أربع جامعات

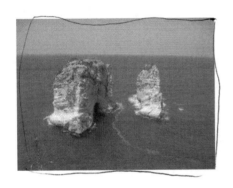

كبار (كبيرة): اللبنانية، إلامريكية، إلعربية،

وإليسوعية. كل أهل لبنان بيعرفوا يئروا (يقرأوا)

ويكتبوا ومعظمون (معظمهم) بيحكوا (يتكلمون)

فرنساوي وانكليزي (فرنسي وانجليزي). اليوم في بلبنان حوالي 34 جامعة معترف فيها.

Lebanon is a small country. Its area is 10,452 square kilometers.

It is well known as a tourist country. Its climate is moderate. It exports fruits and mineral water. Its population is 5 million

people only. Lebanon is not an industrial country because it

does not have large factories. The Lebanese like to travel to

Europe and America. Today they travel to the Arab countries

because there is a lot of work there. There are four major

universities in Lebanon: the Lebanese University, the American

University, the Arab University and the Jesuit University. All the

people of Lebanon know how to read and write and the

majority of them speak French and English. Today, there are 34

accredited universities in Lebanon.

masaaHa =	area	مساحة
mashhoor =	famous	مشهور
siyaaHa =	tourism	سياحة
manaakh =	climate	مناخ

Saddar =	to export	صدّر
fuwaki =	fruit	فواكة
maay =	water	مي
sikkaan =	population	سكّان
a 'daad =	numbers	اعداد
Sinaa 'a =	industry	صناعة
maSna ' =	factory	مصنع
Jaam 'a =	university	جامعة
ma 'daniyyi =	mineral	معدنية

fluel = مَصَكَانِي

Based on the text, answer the following questions:	
shou 'adad sikkaan Libnaan?	What is the number of population in Lebanon?
shou biSaddir?	What does it export?

shou masaaHtu?	What is its area?
Laysh il libnaaniiyii bisaafru labarra? Why do the Lebanese travel abroad?	
kim jaam 'a fee bi libnaan ilyawn? How many universities in Lebanon today?	

شو عدد سكّان لبنان؟
شو بصدّر؟
شو مساحتو؟
ليش اللبنانيي بسافروا لبرا؟
كم جامعة في بلبنان اليوم؟

Lesson Seventeen

L-furṣa khilṣit, w'ana mitl kil-l- ṭullāb rjiʿtʾal jāmʿa. L-yawm awwal dars mnākhdu bi-ṣaf-l-lugha l-ʿarabiyyi l-ʿamiyyi. Ṣār ili shahr ma 'rītʿarabi. Lāzim rāji kil l-drūs illi akhadnāha l-faṣl-l-māḍi hatta itzakkar kil-l-kalimāt wil-jumal. L-furṣa kānit kwaysi. Shift ahli w aṣḥābi. 'Ana ma darast ktīr li'annu ṣadī'i Jamīl ijā min l-maxīk w-bi'i ʾindi tlāt jmāʿ. Halla' lāzim idrus sabʿ sāʿ āt kil yawm ḥatta ma it'akhar bi –drūsi.

1) Conjugate any four verbs of your choice with all pronouns.

2) Make up two sentences using the words: Sha 'b, isti'lāl.

3) The underlined words (in the Arabic Text) are all in plural. Provide the singular of each.

الفرصة خلصت(الفرصة انتهت) وانا متل كل الطلاب، رجعت ع الجامعة ،اليوم أوّل

درس مناخذو بصف اللغة العربية العامية. صار إلي شهر ما أريت(قرأت) عربي،

لازم راجع كل الدروس إلي(التي) أخذناها الفصل الماضي حتى أتذكر كل الكلمات

والجمل. الفرصة كانت كويسة(جيدة)، شفت أهلي وأصحابي، أنا ما درست

كتير(كثير) لأنو(لأنه) صديئي (صديقي) جميل أجا من المكسيك وبئي(وبقي)

عندي تلات (ثلاث) جماع(اسابيع). هلأّ (الآن) لازم ادرس سبع ساعات كل يوم

حتى ما إتأخر (أتأخر) بدروسي.

The break ended, and like all the other students, I returned to

the university. This is the first lesson we take today in the

Arabic dialect class. I have not read Arabic in a month. I must

review all the lessons that we took last semester so I can

remember all the words and sentences. The break was good. I

saw my family and friends. I did not study a lot because my friend Jamil came from Mexico and he stayed with me three weeks. Now I must study seven hours a day in order not to fall behind in my studies.

Hatta ma	in order to	حتى ما
khiliS =	finished – ended	خلص
furSa =	break - vacation	فرصة
Taalib =	student – pupil	طالب
riji' =	returned - to return	رجع
akhad =	he took - to take	اخد
'aammiyyi =	colloquial	عامية

muraaja 'a =	review	مراجعة
Jimli =	sentence	جملة
kilmi =	word	كلمة

dars/ kilmi/ jimli/ SaaHib/ jim 'a/ saa 'a/ – جملة – كلمة – درس

صاحب – جمعة

ساعة –

laysh ana ma darast kteer bil furSa? Why didn't I study a lot

during the break?   ليش انا ما درست كتير بالفرصة؟

Hint = liannu Sadii'i ija min…………

Lesson Eighteen

Mbāriḥ kān arbaᵗāsh kānūn l-tāni mawsim l-shiti wil-talj. Darajit l- ḥarara wiṣlit ᶜashra taḥt l- ṣifr. L-may jalladit wil ṣiyyārāt ma ᶜaadit tdūr. Min-l-saᵗᵗa. law fiyyi ibᵓa bil-bayt w-ma-rūḥ lamaṭraḥ.

Bwalliᶜ l-maw ᵓadi w bishrab nbīd, wib-shūf talifizyon kil-l-nhār. Bas ana lāzim rūḥ ᶜal- ṣaf. Barki yawm l-sabt biᵓdur nām lil-ḍuhur w-mā itruk l-bayt abadan. Min niss sā ᶜa talfan sāḥbi w-āl innū marīḍ. Ṭalab minni khabbir l-istāz innū huwwi mrashshiḥ.

أمبارح كان اربتعش (اربعة عشر) كانون التاني (الثاني) موسم الشتي (الشتاء)

والتلج (الثلج). درجة الحرارة وصلت عشرة تحت الصفر .. المي (المياه) جلّدت

والسيارات ما عادت تدور من الصئعة (الصقيع). لو فيّ ابئا (أبقى) بالبيت وما روح

لمطرَح. بولّع المُوئد (الموقد) وبشرب نبيد وبشوف (أشاهد) تلفزيون كل النهار . بس أنا

لازم روح عالصف. بركي يوم السبت بأدور (اقدر) نام للظهر وما اترك البيت أبداً.

من نص ساعة تلفن(اتصل) صاحبي انو(انه) مريض، وطلب مني خبّر

الاستاز(الأستاذ) انو(انه) هوي(هو) مرشّح.

Yesterday was the 14th of January, the season of winter and

snow. The temperature reached 10 below zero. Water froze

and the cars did not start due to the freezing temperature.

Wish I could stay home and not have to go anywhere. I would

light up the fireplace, drink wine and watch TV all day. But I

must go to class. Perhaps on Saturday, I can sleep until noon

and not leave the house at all. Half an hour ago, my friend

called to say he is sick and he asked me to tell the teacher that

he has a cold.

Maghrour	conceited	مغرور
naam =	slept - to sleep	نام
duhr =	noon	ظهر
SabaaH =	morning	صباح
fajr =	dawn	فجر
Sa' 'a = Saq 'a =	cold	صقعة
bard =	cold	برد
mareedh =	sick	مريض
Talab =	requested	طلب

Istaaz =	teacher	استاز
mrashshaH =	has a cold	مرشّح
Sifr =	zero	صفر
Jallad =	froze	جلّد
taHt =	under – below	تحت
faw' =	above - over	فوق
siyyara =	car	سيارة
daarit =	turned on - started	دارت
maw 'id =	date - appointment	موعد
nbeed =	wine	نبيد

Who is your favorite actor?	Meen huwwi mumathilak al mufadhal?
	مين هو ممثلك المفضل؟
what are the 12 months of the year in order.	shou hiyyi shour alsini?
	شو هيي شهور السنة؟
what are the four seasons?	shou hiyyi al fuSul al arba 'a?
	شو هيي الفصول الأربعة؟
What is your favorite season?	shou huwwi faSlak al mufadhal?
	شو هوي فصلك المفضل؟
What are your hobbies?	shou hiyii hiwaayatak?
	شو هيي هواياتك؟
Why didn't the cars start?	laysh ma daarit al siyyaaraat?
	ليش ما دارت السيارات؟
What do I want to do on Saturday?	shou baddi a 'mil yawm al sabt?
	شو بدي اعمل يوم السبت؟

Lesson Nineteen

Kān ʿindi sayyāra ʿatīʾa btākhud banzīn ktīr. Wil-frām fiya rakhu. Inkasarit limrāyi l-idmāniyyi win-fakhat l-dūlāb. Kamān nkasar l-ashikmān. Biʿ ta wishtarayt siyyāra jdīdi. ʿarabīyti lawna azraʾ modāl l- aʾlfayan w-tisʿa mistawradi min ilmānia. Siʿ ra ʿashr tālāf dolār. Baddi sūʾa ana w-khayyi tānzūr ibnʿ ammi. Ana bHib l-swāʾa khāssatan ʿal-autostrād liʾannū mā fi adwiyi wlā kwāʿ.

كان عندي سيارة عتيئة(عتيقة) بتاخذ(تأخذ) بنزين كتير(كثير)، والفرام(الفرامل) فيا(فيها) رخو . انكسرت المراية الادمانيه(الأمامية) وانفخت الدولاب، كمان(ايضاً) انكسر الاشكمان. بعتا(بعت) وشتريت سيارة جديدة(جديدة). عربيتي(سيارتي) لونا أزرء(ازرق) مودال الألفين وتسعة مستوردة من ألمانيا. سعرا(سعرها)عشر تلاف دولار(عشرة ألاف) بدي (اريد) سوءا(أسوقها) أنا وخيّ(وأخي) تتنزور(حتى نزور) ابن عمي. أنا بحب السواءة خاصة عل أوتوستراد لانو(لأنه) ما في اضوية(اضواء) ولا كواع.

203

I had an old car that consumed a lot of gasoline and the break was loose. The front mirror broke and the tire had a hole and the muffler broke. I sold it and bought a new car. The color of my car is blue and it is a 2009 model imported from Germany. Its price is ten thousand dollars. I want to drive it with my brother in order to visit my cousin. I like driving especially on the highway because it has no traffic lights and no turns.

mustawrad =	imported	مستورد
daw =	light	ضو
koo ' =	turn – curve	كوع
ishtara =	bought - to buy	اشترى
baa ' =	sold - to sell	باع
asra ' =	faster	اسرع
'atii'a =	old	عتيقة
fraam =	brake	فرام
rakhu =	loose	رخو
mraayyi =	mirror	مراية

doulaab =	tire – wheel	دولاب
inkasar =	broke	انكسر
infakhat =	had a hole	انفخت
ashikmaan =	muffler	اشكمان
'arabiyyi =	car	عربيّة
siyyara =	car	سيارة
laoun =	color	لون
azraq =	blue	أزرق
alfayn =	two thousand	الفين
ilmaaniya =	Germany	المانيا
benzene =	gasoline	بنزين

Based on the text, answer the following questions:
shou lawn siyyarti li jdeedi?   What is the color of my new car?

شو لون سيارتي الجديدة؟	
min ay balad hiyyi?	من أي بلد Which country it is from? هيي؟
meen baddu yisouq ma 'i?	مين بدو who will drive with me? يسوقا معي؟
lawayn badna nrouH?	لوين بدنا نروح؟ Where will we go?
laysh bHib al autostraad?	ليش Why do I like the highway? بحب الاوتوستراد؟
shou inkasar bil siyyara al 'ateeqa?	What broke in the old car? شو انكسر بالسيارة العتيقة؟
shou infakhat?	What had a hole? شو انفخت؟

Lesson Twenty

Ana lāzim 'uṣ shaʿrī , bayyi alli innū shaʿri ṭawīl. Talfant lil-ḥillāʾ ta-ākhud mawʿid minnū . Mbāriḥ kān mashghūl. Riḥt ʿind hillāʾ tāni w aṣṣayt shaʿrī. Lbist tyābi l-jdād w riḥt ʿa-ḥafli maʿ rfīʾtī. Bʾīna lis-sā ʿa tnayn. Niḥnā w-rājʿ īn ṣār maʿnā ḥādis ʾaw (accidān). Hiyyi kasarit ijra w-anā jaraḥt wijji. Akhadūnaʿ al-mistashfa w-ʿimlū ʿamaliyyi (li-rfīʾti). Hallaʾ ṣirna aḥsan. Hiyyi sār fiya timshi w-ana shālu l-iṭab ʿan wijji.

أنا لازم أُص(اقص) شعري، بيي ألّي انو شعري طويل. تلفنت للحلاء(للحلاق)

تآخد(تأخذ) موعد منّو(منه). أمبارح كان مشغول، رحت عند حلاء تاني(ثاني)

وأصيت(قصيت) شعري. لبست تياب(ثياب) الجداد(الجدد) ورحت عَ حفلة مع

رفيئتي(رفيقتي) بإينا(بقينا) لسّاعة تنين. نحنا وراجعين صار معنا حادس(حادث) أو

أكسيدان. هيي(هي) كسرت إجرا، وأنا جرحت وجي(وجهي).أخدونا(أخذونا) عَ

207

المستشفى وعملوا عملية لِرفيئتي(لرفيقتي). هلأ صرنا أحسن هيي صار فيا تمشي

وأنا شالو الئطب(القطب)عن وجّي(وجهي).

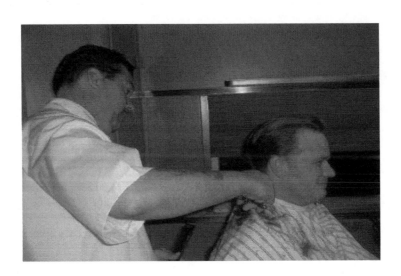

I must have a haircut. My father told me that my hair is long. I called the barber yesterday to get an appointment from him. He was busy. I went to another barber and had a haircut. I wore my new clothes and went to a party with my girlfriend. We stayed until two o'clock. On the way back, we had an accident. She broke her leg and I had a cut on my face. They took us to the hospital and operated on my girlfriend. Now we are better. She can now walk, and they removed the stiches from my face.

Koloniya	perfume	كولونيا
'iyaadi	clinic	عيادي
tiyaab =	clothes	تياب
Ijr =	leg	اجر
wijj =	face	وج – وجه
Hafli =	party	حفلة
biqi =	remain	بقي
tnayn =	two	تنين
rfeeqa =	friend (girl)	رفيقة
mistashfa =	hospital	مستشفى

qiTab =	stitches	قطب
'amaliyyi =	operation	عملية
hala' =	now	هلق
shaal =	to remove	شال
libis =	to wear	لبس
riHt =	I went to	رحت
mashghool =	busy	مشغول
mbaariH =	yesterday	مبارح
minnu =	from him	منّو
maw 'id =	appointment	موعد

Hillaaq =	barber	حلاق
sha 'r =	hair	شعر
uss =	cut	اص – قصّ

Based on the text, answer the following questions:

meen aal sha 'ri Taweel?	Who said that my hair is long?

مين قال شعري طويل؟

meen kaan mashgoul mbaariH?	Who was busy yesterday?

مين كان مشغول مبارح

wayn assayt sha 'ri?	Where did I have a hair cut?

وين قصيت شعري؟

Laysh l bist tyaab jdaad? Why did I wear new clothes? ليش لبست تياب جداد؟	
ijr meen inkasarit? Whose leg was broken? اجر مين انكسرت؟	
meen 'imil 'amaliyyi? Who had an operation? مين عمل عملية؟	
meen akhadna 'al mistashfaa? Who took us to the hospital? مين اخدنا عالمستشفى؟	

Lesson Twenty-One

Ana w-marti w-ikhti riḥna ʿal mathaf l-brī ṭāni ta-nitfarraj ʿal-
lawḥāt. Il-binā̄yyi arbaʿ ṭawābiʾ w-fiyā asonser.(misʿad). Fitnaʿ
a-awwal ṭābiʾ w-shifna rasmāt min l-arn l-sādis ʿashr. Baʿd ma
aḍḍayna ḥawāli l-sāʿ tayn kinna taʿ bānīn min l-mashi. Riḥna
bil-siyyāra tanzūr baytʿammi. Martʿammi kānitʿam tijli. W-ʿ
ammiʿam yisʾi l-zhūr bil-jnayni. Wiṣil ṣihri w-maʿ u wlādū.
itʿashshayna kilna hawnīk w-lamma khliṣna akalna fwāki w-
kil wāḥad rāh ʿa-baytu.

أنا ومرتي وأختي رحنا عَ المتحف البريطاني تا نتفرج عَ اللوحات، البناية اربع

طوابئ(طوابق)، وفيا آسنسار(مصعد)، فتنا عَ أول طابئ(طابق) وشفنا

رسمات(رسومات) من الأرن(القرن) السادس عشر . بعد ما أضّينا(قضينا) حوالي

الساعتين كنا تعبانين من المشي، رحنا بالسيارة تنزور بيت عمي. مرت عمي كانت

عم تجلي وعمي عم يسئي(يسقى) الزهور بالجنيني. وصل صهري ومعو ولادو

(أولاده). إتعشينا كلنا هونيك ولما خلصنا أكلنا فواكي (فواكهة)، وكل واحد راح ع

بيتو .

My wife, my sister and I went to the British Museum to look at the paintings. The building has four floors and an elevator. We entered the first floor and saw paintings from the sixteenth century. After we spent around two hours, we were tired of walking. We went by car to visit my uncle's house. My aunt was washing dishes and my uncle was watering the flowers in the garden. My brother-in-law arrived with his kids. We all had dinner there. After dinner we ate fruit and everyone went home.

Issit Hubb	love story	قصة حب
marti –	my wife	مرتي
matHaf –	museum	متحف
breeTani -	British	بريطاني
nitfarraj -	to look at	نتفرج
lawHa –	painting	لوحة
binaayi	building	بناية
Taabi'/ Tawaabi'	floor (s)	طابق
asansar/miS 'ad	elevator	اسانسور – مصعد
arn/qarn	century	قرن

saadis 'ashar –	sixteenth	سادس عشر
ti 'baan –	tired	تعبان
mashi	walking	مشي
ziyaara	visit	زيارة
'am tijli –	washing dishes	عم تجلي
'am yisqi -	watering	عم يسقي
zhour –	flowers	زهور
Jnayni	garden	نينة
Sihri –	my brother-in-law	صهري
hawneek	there	هونيك

hawn -	here	هون
fwaaki	fruit	فواكه
raaH	went	راح

Based on the text answer the following questions:
meen raaH 'al matHaf? Who went to the museum? مين راح ع المتحف؟
ayya matHaf?   Which museum?   ايا متحف؟
lashou riHna?   Why did we go?   لشو رحنا؟
kim Taabi' l binaayyi? How many floors in the building? كم طابق البناية؟

البناية؟	
niHna halla' bi ayya arn? Which century are we in now? نحن هلق بأيا أرن؟	
shou kaanit 'am ta 'mil mart 'ammi? What was my aunt doing? شو كانت عمتعمل مرت عمي؟	
w 'ammi kaan..? And my uncle was..? وعمي كان؟	
meen ija kamaan? Who also came? مين اجا كمان؟	

Lesson Twenty-Two

Baʿ d arbaʿ jimaʿ bīṣīr l-ṭaʾs aḥsan. Ākhir jimʿ a min niisān ʿiid l-shaʿnīni, w baʿd arbaʿ jimaʿ ʿid l-kbīr. Bil-nisbi lil muʿtaʾad l-masīḥi, hayda aham ʿīd. Liʾannū ʿīd l-īyāmi. Baʿd l-ʿazāb wil ṣalb, wil mawt, byiji yawm l-baʿth. ʾuṣṭurit l-baʿth mhimmi ktīr bil-adab l-ʿarabi l-hadīth. Muʿzam l-shuʿara istaghalūha bi-shiʿrun w-dāfu ila min adab l-yūnān wil-ādāb l-ʿālamiyi. L-adab l-ʿarabi l-yawm aṣʿab ktīr min adab l-ʿuṣūr l-wusṭa. Liʾannū l-shāʿir l-muʿāṣir ʿindu saʾāfī wāsʿa wib- yaʿrif aktar min lugha wiḥdi, w byistakhdim asālīb min adab l-gharb.

بعد أربع جمع بصير الطئس(الطقس) أحسن. آخر جمعه من نيسان عيد الشعنيني،

وبعد أربع جمع عيد الكبير. بالنسبه للمعتئد(بالنسبة للمعتقد) المسيحي، هيدا أهم

عيد. لأنو عيد الإيامي(القيامة). بعد العَزاب(العذاب) والصلب، والموت. بيجي يوم

البعث. اسطورت(اسطورة) البعث مهمه(مهمة) كتير بالأدب العربي

الحديس(الحديث). معظم الشعرا استغلوها بِشعرن وضافوا إلها من أدب اليونان

219

والآداب العالمية. الأدب العربي اليوم أصعب كتير من أدب العصور الوسطى. لأنو الشاعر المعاصر عندو سآفي(ثقافة) واسعة وبيعرف اكتر من لغة واحدة و بيستخدم اساليب مأخودي من أدب الغرب.

In four weeks the weather will improve. The last week of April is Palm Sunday and four weeks later is Easter Sunday. According to the Christian belief, this is the most important holiday because it is the Feast of the Resurrection. After suffering, crucifixion and death, there comes the Day of Resurrection. The myth of rebirth is very important in Modern Arabic Literature. Most poets utilized it in their poetry and they added to it from the Greek and other world literatures. Today, Arabic Literature is more difficult than Medieval Literature because the contemporary poet has a wide education, knows more than one language and employs styles derived from Western Literature.

ightiSaab	rape	اغتصاب
biSeer –	becomes	بيصير
Taqs –	weather	طقس
Jim 'a/ osbou ' -	week	جمعة – اسبوع

yawm	day	يوم
'iid –	festivity	عيد
sha 'nini –	palm Sunday	شعنيني
'iid l kibeer -	Easter	عيد الكبير
mu 'taqad -	belief	معتقد
maseeHi –	Christian	مسيحي
muslim –	Islamic	مسلم
aham –	most important	اهم
qiyaami	resurrection	قيامة
'azaab	suffering	عزاب

Salb	crucifixion	صلب
mawt	death	موت
ba 'th	rebirth	بعث
usTura -	myth	اسطورة
adab –	literature	ادب
hadeeth –	modern	حديث
adeem	old/ancient	قديم
mu 'zam –	most of	معظم
shaa 'ir -	poet	شاعر
shu 'ara –	poets	شعرا

istaghall	to exploit	استغل
adhaaf	added	اضاف
yunaani	Greek	يوناني
'aalami -	world/international	عالمي
aS 'ab	harder	أصعب
al 'uSur al wusTa	Middle Ages	العصور الوسطى
mu 'aaSir -	contemporary	معاصر
saqaafi	culture	ثقافة
lugha -	language	لغة
istakhdam –	used	استخدم

asaaleeb	styles/ methods	اساليب
al gharb -	the West	الغرب

Based on the text, answer the following questions:
ayya 'iid bi aakhir nisaan?   What festivity is at the end of April?   أيا عيد بآخر نيسان؟
W ba 'du ayy 'iid?   And after it, what comes? وبعدو أيا عيد؟
Laysh 'iid l kbeer muhim kteer? Why is Easter very important?   ليش عيد الكبير مهم كتير؟
shou byiji ba 'd l mawt?   What comes after death? شو بيجي بعد الموت؟

الموت؟
ay usTura istaghallu l shu 'ara? What myth did the poets exploit? أي أسطورة استغلوا الشعرا؟
min wayn daafu ilha? From where did they add to it? من وين ضافوا الها؟
Shou 'indu l shaa 'ir l mu 'aaSir? What does the contemporary poet has? شو عندو الشاعر المعاصر؟
shou biya 'rif kamaan? What else does he know? شو بيعرف كمان؟؟

Lesson Twenty-Three

Bayrūt min ajmal mudun l-shar' l-awsaṭ. Lākin bil-ṣayf shawb ktīr. Sikkān   l-ʿāṣmi l-libnāniyi bīrūhū ʿal baḥr aw ʿal jabal. Hinni tlāt a'sām. 'Usm bī 'aḍḍu l-ṣayf ʿal baḥr. Bīrūḥū kil yawm, aw byista'jru shāleh. Shaṭ Bayrūt mashhūr ʿal-baḥr l-abyaḍ l-muṭawassiṭ. Usm byista'jru bayt bil jabal li'annū l-manākh aḥsan, wi l-ṭa's abrad. w-usm biḍallu bi-shighlun, lākin bi-ʿiṭlit l-usbūʿ bīrūḥū ʿal baḥr aw ʿal jabal byākhdu ghurfi bil-otāl lamiddit yawmayn.

بيروت من أجمل مدن الشرء(الشرق) الأوسط. لكن بالصيف شوب كتير . سكان

العاصمة اللبنانبة بيروحوا ع البحر أو ع الجبل. هنّي تلات(ثلاث) أئسام(أقسام):

أسم(قسم) بأضّوا الصيف ع البحر، بيروحوا كل يوم أو بيستئجروا(يستأجرون) شاليه.

شط بيروت مشهور ع البحر الأبيض المتوسط. أسم(قسم) بيستئجروا بيت بالجبل

لأنو المناخ أحسن، والطئس(الطقس) أبرد. وأسم بيظلوا بشغلون لكن بعطلة الأسبوع

بيروحوا ع البحر أو ع الجبل بياخدوا غرفي(غرفة) بالأوتيل لمدة يومين.

Beirut is one of the most beautiful cities of the Middle East. But

in the summer, it is too hot. The inhabitants of the Lebanese

capital go to the sea or to the mountain. The people are of

three groups: one group spends the summer on the beach; they

go every day or they rent a cabin there. Beirut's shore is famous

on the Mediterranean. Another group rents a house in the

mountain because the climate is better and the weather is
cooler. A group remains at work, but on the weekend they go
to the beach or to the mountain. They take a room in a hotel
for two days.

jabal –	mountain	جبل
'uTlit l ousbou '	weekend	عطلة الاسبوع
qism/ism -	part/group	قسم
Jameel	beautiful	جميل
ajmal –	more beautiful	أجمل
madeeni –	city	مدينة
'aaSmi -	capital	عاصمة

shawb/Harr -	hot	شوب – حرّ
Ista'jar -	to rent	استأجر
Jameel	beautiful	جميل
ajmal –	more beautiful	أجمل
madeeni –	city	مدينة
'aaSmi -	capital	عاصمة
shawb/Harr -	hot	شوب – حرّ
Ista'jar -	to rent	استأجر

Ishtara -	to buy	اشترى
baa ' -	to sell	باع
ghurfi -	room	غرفة
shaT - شطّ	sea shore	
manaakh –	climate	مناخ
abrad -	cooler	أبرد
ajmal –	more beautiful	اجمل
aHsan -	better	أحسن

Taqs -	weather	طقس
middit -	period of time	مدة
yawm –	one day	يوم
yawmayn –	two days	يومين

Based on the text, answer the following questions:

shou 'aaSmit Libnaan? What is the capital of Lebanon? شو

عاصمة

keef Ta's Beirut bil Sayf? How is Beirut's weather in the

summer?   كيف طقس بيروت بالصيف؟

shou 'aaSmit Libnaan? What is the capital of Lebanon? شو

عاصمة لبنان؟

keef Ta's Beirut bil Sayf? How is Beirut's weather in the

summer?كيف طقس بيروت بالصيف؟

keef Ta's Beirut bil Sayf? How is Beirut's weather in the

summer?كيف طقس بيروت بالصيف؟

wayn bi ruHu l sikkaan bil Sayf? Where do the residents go in

the summer?وين بيروحوا السكان بالصيف؟

233

shaTT Beirut 'a ayya BaHr? At which sea lies Beirut's coast? شط بيروت ع ايا بحر؟

laysh biruHu l naas 'al jabal? Why do the people go to the mountain?ليش بيروحوا الناس ع الجبل؟

shou biya 'mlu l naas bi 'uTlit l ousbou '? What do people do in the weekend?شو بيعملوا الناس بعطلة الاسبوع؟

Lesson Twenty-Four
(A poem by the author of the book)

Jawāb l-layl

Sa'alt l-layl 'an ḥilwi sabiyyi

Jadāyil sha'arha sūd w-'abāya

Ṣār l-lāyl yitḍaḥḥak 'alayyi

W'alli rūḥ nisyūk l- Ṣabāya

Ṣārit 'ishtak su' bi shwayyi

La shfāf wla'yūn wla hadāya

Mā bīhimni ma dām hiyyi

w'ana 'aṭūl Ṣaffayna l-nawāya

Hiyyi arāyibi w-immi w-bayyi

Fidāha kil amwāl l-barāya

Ḥatta rmūshha b-albi tfayyi

Bikhṭi ad ma badda khaṭāya
Ri'it Ṣawtha fiha n̄ūmiyyi
lān l- Ṣakhr wi'lūb l-awāya
w law kil-l-bashar ḍiḥku ʿalayyi

w'ālu ḥubha ʿaks l-waṢāya
Bitruk jannit l-khild l-haniyyi

wmā binsa laḥzit l-kānit maʿāya.

جواب الليل

سألت الليل عن حلوة صبية

جدايل شعرها سود وعبايا

صار الليل يتضحك عليّ

وألي روح نِسيوك الصبايا

صارت عيشتك صعبة شويه

لا شفاف ولا عيون ولا هدايا

ما بيهمني ما دام هيي

وأنا عا طول صفيّنا النوايا

هيي أرايبي وإمي وبيي

فيداها كل أموال البرايا

حتى رموشها بئلبي تفيي

بِخطي أد ما بدّها خطايا

رئَّة(رقة) صوتها فيها نعُومِّيه

لان إلصخر وألوب الأوايا

ولو كل الّبشر ضحكوا عليّ

وآلوا حبها عكس الوصايا

بترك جنة الخلد الهنية

وما بنسا لحظة الكانت معايا

Jawaab –	answer	جواب
Su'aal -	question	سؤال
Layl -	night	ليل
Sabiyyi -	young woman	صبيّة
Jadaayel -	locks of hair	جدايل
Sha 'r -	hair	شَعر

maghroom faw' raasu	over his head in love	مغروم فوق راسو
Soud -	black	سود
'abaaya -	thick	عبايا
dhiHik -	laughed	ضحك
'alayyi -	at me	عليي
nisi -	forgot	نسي

Sa 'b -	difficult	صعب
shouwayi	a little	شويي
shfaaf -	lips	شفاف
'uyoun	eyes	عيون
hadaaya	gifts	هدايا
ma daam	as long as	ما دام

nawaaya –	intentions	نوايا
araayib –	relatives	ارايب
maal -	money	مال
rimsh –	eye lashes	رمش
khaTiyyi -	sin	خطيي
SawT -	voice	صوت

n ʻumiyyyi -	tenderness	نعوميي
Sakhr -	rock	صخر
alb/qalb -	heart	قلب
awi/qawi -	strong	قوي
bashar –	people	بشر
dhiHik -	laghed	ضحك

waSaaya -	commandments	وصايا
Janni	paradise	جنّة

About the Author

George Nicolas El-Hage, Ph.D. is a Lebanese-American poet, professor, linguist, administrator and writer. He was born in Mansourieh El-Metn, Lebanon in 1952. His father was Nicolas Iskandar El-Hage and his mother was Martha Abounader El-Hage. Dr. El-Hage completed his elementary and secondary school education in Lebanon. He acquired his B.A. in Arabic Literature from the Lebanese University in Beirut, Lebanon. While in Beirut, El-Hage studied with and was influenced by poets like Buland al-Haidari and Khalil Hawi. He then emigrated to the United States where he completed both his Master of Arts and Ph.D. in Arabic and Comparative Literature at the State University of New York in Binghamton. His dissertation (later published into a book by NDU Press, Lebanon) was on William Blake and Kahlil Gibran: Poets of Prophetic Vision. He has taught at Yale University, Binghamton University, The Lebanese University, Columbia University, the Monterey Institute of International Studies (a graduate school of Middlebury College) and the Defense Language Institute. His academic career has been equally spent between teaching, authoring, lecturing and administration.

Dr. El-Hage is a prolific writer with a perfect command of both English and Arabic languages. His training and expertise in the field of Arabic and Comparative Literature has enabled him to delve into a wide range of topics and areas covering literature, mythology, mysticism, language acquisition, criticism, theology and art. He is a published poet in Arabic, both in Modern Standard and in spoken Levantine Dialect as well as in Lebanese Zajal. He also writes poetry in English and is an accomplished translator.

Dr. El-Hage has published seven volumes of poetry, numerous research articles, books on language pedagogy and poetry in Lebanese Dialect and Zajal. His poetry betrays a marked fluctuation between a deep romantic sensitivity and a tragic existential awareness which colors his reading of current universal and regional events. The tragedy of his embattled country constitutes a dominant theme in his writings. El-Hage is a supporter of the free verse movement in Modern Arabic Poetry. Nevertheless, he still appreciates the Qasida 'Amudiyya, the classical form of traditional Arabic Poetry. He always chooses short meters, and his poetry is characterized by its musical effects.

Made in the USA
San Bernardino, CA
02 February 2017